BANKING THE FURNACE

Restructuring of the Steel Industry in Eight Countries

Trevor Bain
University of Alabama

1992

W.E. UPJOHN INSTITUTE for Employment Research
Kalamazoo, Michigan

Library of Congress Cataloging-in-Publication Data

Bain, Trevor.
    Banking the furnace : restructuring of the steel industry in eight
countries / Trevor Bain.
        p.   cm.
    Includes bibliographical references and index.
    ISBN 0-88099-128-3. — ISBN 0-88099-127-5 (pbk.)
    1. Steel industry and trade.   2. Collective bargaining—Steel
industry and trade.   3. Corporate reorganizations.   I. Title.
HD9510.5.B25   1992
338.4'7669142—dc20   92-18358
                                                                              CIP

Cover design by J.R. Underhill.
Index prepared by Shirley Kessel.
Printed in the United States of America.

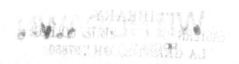

ACKNOWLEDGMENTS

The genesis of this project was a sabbatical semester in Europe during the fall of 1982, with assistance from the Carl Duisberg Society. At that time Bob Aronson, Bob McKersie and Lloyd Ulman encouraged me to pursue a comparative study of steel industry restructuring at the shop-floor level. Continued financial support was provided by the John R. Miller Professorship, the University of Alabama's Research Grants committee, and the College of Commerce and Business Administration. Subsequently, financial support received from the W.E. Upjohn Institute for Employment Research allowed me to greatly expand the scope of the research, and finally, the Rockefeller Foundation scholar's program in Bellagio, Italy provided the uninterrupted time to complete a first draft.

I am particularly grateful to a legion of union officials, industrial relations managers, government officials, works council members, and academics who gave freely of their time in each country and provided me with most of the material for this monograph. They taught me something about comparative labor relations and cheerfully read drafts of earlier papers.

I have been fortunate to have a group of able graduate assistants who aided in the research. I thank Martin Abercrombie, Edwin Arnold, Cathy Blakeslee, Jana Kuzmicki, Chris Lowery, Jim Simpson, Meera Venkatachalam, and particularly David Williams, who wrote the Fairfield Case.

While my research was in progress, I discussed the findings in seminars at Cornell University and the University of California—Los Angeles. I am grateful to Roy Adams, T.V. Eason, Robert Flanagan, K.M. Jackson, Herbert Morton, Hans Mueller, Keith Sisson, and John Windmuller, all of whom reviewed sections of the first draft. Several members of the Upjohn Institute provided support. Allan Hunt shepherded the entire project, Lou Jacobson read the entire first and second drafts and provided numerous suggestions that pushed me to sharpen the analysis, and Judy Gentry lent editorial assistance.

Several drafts of the text were processed by an able department staff, including Mary Burnett, Lucille Maranda, Lisa Patrick, Margaret Perdue, and Mary Jane Taylor. They are the only people in the world who can read my handwriting.

Finally, I owe the greatest debt to my wife Helena, who often waited beyond reason for me in some city while I concluded just one more interview and then proceeded with enthusiasm to introduce me to other aspects of each culture.

THE AUTHOR

Trevor Bain is John R. Miller Professor and Director of the Human Resources Institute in the Manderson Graduate School of Business, University of Alabama. He received his BA from the City College of New York, MILR from Cornell University, and Ph.D. from the University of California—Berkeley. He has held teaching appointments at Queens College of CUNY, the University of Michigan, and the University of Arizona.

Professor Bain's primary research interests have focused on restructuring and technological change, public employment programs, scientific and technical manpower, and comparative labor relations. He has published extensively in such journals as *Industrial Relations, Academy of Management Review, Columbia Journal of World Business,* and *Kyklos.* He is the recipient of research awards from many organizations, including the U.S. Department of Labor, the National Science Foundation, the Ford Foundation, and the Rockefeller Foundation. Professor Bain is also an active arbitrator.

CONTENTS

TABLES

FIGURES

BANKING THE FURNACE

**Restructuring of
the Steel Industry
in Eight Countries**

1
Introduction

Prior to the 1970s, the industrialized countries enjoyed more than two decades of almost uninterrupted prosperity. Labor and management participated in a social contract which allowed each to improve its position while government policies assisted both parties. The end of this unprecedented post-war boom coincided with oil price increases, competition from newly developing countries, and a decline in demand for heavy capital goods. The new competitive environment challenged the steel industry and placed stress on the relationships between labor, management, and government.

The purpose of this study is to examine how the cross-national differences in the social contract among managers, unions, and government influenced adjustment strategies in steel. The restructuring process in eight major steel-producing countries, categorized as having either an adversarial or a cooperative industrial relations system, are studied in order to determine who bore the costs of restructuring— employers, employees, or government—and which industrial relations systems were more efficient in restructuring. The study postulates that restructuring was more heavily influenced by market forces and new technology than by collective bargaining and bargaining power; however, the nature of the social contract determined who bore the costs of restructuring.

The steel industry presents an excellent opportunity for a comparative study because the industry is international in its technology, choice of products, raw materials and markets. Steelmaking technology crosses national boundaries easily, and the product is undifferentiated, which permits international competition. The steel unions have traditionally been among the most powerful in every industrial relations system. The eight countries chosen for this study—Belgium, Canada, Germany, Great Britain, Japan, Luxembourg, Sweden, and the United States—are meant to be representative rather than inclusive of the major steel producing countries. France and Italy would be included in a larger study, while important steel producers such as the former Soviet Union and China would be excluded, because they do not meet

the criteria of possessing democratic unions and market driven economies.

The crisis in steel among the world's industrialized countries
became obvious after 1974. By the late 1960s, important infrastructure
in the western countries had been completed, and a sharp reduction in
steel consumption occurred in 1968-69. Even without the oil shocks of
1973-1974, steel demand would not have continued its earlier rising
trend (Barnett and Schorsch 1983; Scheuerman 1986; Meny and
Wright 1986). Table 1.1 presents data on crude steel production for the
eight countries in this study. These eight countries produced more than
half (54 percent) of the world's steel in 1970, but a little more than one-
third (37 percent) by 1990 (OECD 1991). During those two decades,
world steel production had expanded, but these eight countries had not
shared equally in the market increase. Instead, they were forced to
restructure their steel industries, reduce capacity, and shed jobs. Since
1970, 52 percent of the steel jobs in the eight countries have been eliminated (see table 1.2).

Several environmental changes explain the crisis in steel during the
1970s and 1980s. There was a secular decline in the demand for steel
due to the changing demand for the products. As economies matured,
the relative position of heavy steel-intensive industries, such as shipbuilding and railroads, gave way to growth industries, such as space
technology, telecommunications, and biotechnology, which use little
steel. Steel was also being replaced by aluminum, plastics, resistant
glass and ceramics. This was particularly true for automobiles, long the
major customer for the integrated steel companies. At the same time,
new competition developed; Japan entered in the 1960s, followed by
South Korea, Brazil, Venezuela, India and Mexico. For these new competitors, steel consumption accelerates above a national income of
about $500 per capita, and higher levels of capital formation in infra-
structure were reinforced by demand within a growing manufacturing
sector (Aylen 1983). After 1974, the post oil-shock world recession
also affected the demand for heavy capital goods. Demand declined at
that time, particularly in the automobile industry as automakers sought
to substantially lighten their vehicles in response to rising fuel prices.

Additional causes of the steel crisis included improper investment
policies, lagging technological change, increased import penetration,
and increased capacity.

At the same time that the steel industry in the eight countries faced a crisis, their industrial relations systems were also under stress. Industrial relations had enjoyed a measure of stability following the Second World War when managers, employees and their unions, and government each recognized their position in the social contract forged by the need to rebuild their economies. Among the largest and strongest unions were the metalworkers and steelworkers, who had negotiated high wages for their members. Kassalow (1984) placed the steelworkers' compensation at twice the average U.S. manufacturing employee, 22 percent above average British workers, and 9 percent above average German workers. However, the new competitive environment placed stress on the relationship among the three actors. Layoffs and plant shutdowns created a harsher negotiating climate, and unions were asked to accept wage freezes, reductions in benefits and the loss of their members jobs (Kochan, Katz, and McKersie 1987). At the same time that the bargaining relationship was changing, the political power of the unions was diminished as parliamentary governments, which had previously supported the unions, became more conservative.

The theoretical framework of the study (see figure 1.1) is based on the traditional collective bargaining model, with the difference that the bargaining process and bargaining power are assumed to be environmental forces. Economic factors, the organizational and institutional context, sociodemographic factors, and the legal environment affect restructuring outcomes. This framework relies heavily on the work of the Webbs (1897), Commons (1934), Perlman (1928), and Dunlop (1958). However, it differs from their work in one important respect. The goals and strategies of employers, employees and their unions, and government are important environmental factors which affect outcomes. Borrowing from the work of Kochan, McKersie, and Cappelli (1984), the bargaining process in this model goes beyond the traditional activities of negotiating over wages, hours, and employment to include strategic decisions such as type of products, the size of the company, and new technology.

The form of structural adjustment discussed in this study may be termed internal. Adjustment is carried out within the industry and often within a firm or plant by the introduction of new products, a different mix of products, the introduction of new technology, improved utilization of plant equipment and human resources, and the dismantling of

Table 1.1
Crude Steel Production in Eight Countries, 1970-1990
(millions of metric tons)

Year	Adversarial			Cooperative				Total
	Canada	Great Britain	United States	Belgium and Luxembourg	Germany	Japan	Sweden	
1970	11.20	28.33	119.31	18.07	45.04	93.32	5.50	320.77
1971	11.04	24.15	109.26	17.69	40.31	88.56	5.27	296.28
1972	11.86	25.28	120.87	19.99	43.71	96.90	5.26	323.87
1973	13.39	26.65	136.80	21.45	49.52	119.32	5.66	372.79
1974	13.62	22.38	132.20	22.67	53.23	117.13	5.99	367.22
1975	13.03	19.78	105.82	16.21	40.42	102.31	5.61	303.18
1976	13.29	22.40	116.12	16.71	42.42	107.40	5.14	323.48
1977	13.63	20.47	113.70	15.59	38.99	102.41	3.97	308.76
1978	14.90	20.30	124.31	17.39	41.25	102.11	4.33	324.59
1979	16.05	21.47	123.69	18.39	46.04	111.75	4.73	342.12
1980	15.90	11.28	101.46	16.94	43.84	111.40	4.24	305.06
1981	14.81	15.32	109.61	16.07	41.61	101.68	3.77	302.87
1982	11.87	13.74	67.66	13.50	35.88	99.55	3.90	246.10
1983	12.83	14.98	76.76	13.45	35.73	97.18	4.21	255.14
1984	14.70	15.21	83.94	15.29	39.39	105.59	4.71	278.83

1985	14.64	15.77	80.07	14.63	40.50	105.28	4.81	275.70
1986	14.08	14.77	74.03	13.42	37.13	98.28	4.71	256.42
1987	14.74	17.14	80.88	13.09	36.25	98.51	4.60	265.21
1988	15.19	19.07	90.65	14.90	41.03	105.68	4.78	291.30
1989	15.46	18.80	88.43	14.70	41.07	107.91	4.69	291.06
1990	12.28	17.92	88.90	15.03	38.43	110.33	4.45	287.34
1970-1990								
Absolute change	1.08	-10.41	-30.41	-3.04	-6.61	17.01	-1.05	-33.43
Percentage change	9.64	-36.75	-25.49	-16.82	-14.68	18.23	-19.09	-10.42

SOURCE: OECD printout, Paris, 1991.

Table 1.2
Total Employment in Steel in Eight Countries, 1970-1990
(thousands)

Year	Adversarial				Cooperative			Total
	Canada	Great Britain	United States	Belgium and Luxembourg	Germany	Japan	Sweden	
1970	47.5	222.4	549.6	82.6	237.7	345.2	41.0	1,526.0
1971	47.0	207.5	506.8	82.5	231.0	350.8	n.a.	1,425.6[a]
1972	50.0	200.9	496.7	82.9	222.0	339.7	n.a.	1,392.2[a]
1973	45.5	196.2	521.7	85.6	228.4	325.2	n.a.	1,402.6[a]
1974	52.5	197.7	522.6	86.6	230.6	323.9	51.6	1,465.4
1975	51.5	183.1	470.1	80.8	221.9	324.4	45.8	1,377.6
1976	49.7	183.3	469.9	80.4	220.3	320.3	44.1	1,368.0
1977	49.7	182.0	469.9	74.3	214.4	314.8	41.4	1,346.5
1978	52.7	165.4	472.0	65.3	202.8	302.5	39.1	1,299.8
1979	53.0	156.4	478.5	65.0	204.8	281.5	39.0	1,278.2
1980	53.2	112.1	429.3	60.1	197.4	271.0	38.3	1,161.4
1981	53.0	88.2	423.6	57.5	186.7	269.3	35.8	1,114.1
1982	43.0	74.5	323.6	54.1	175.9	268.5	33.6	973.2
1983	42.0	63.7	340.8	52.5	163.7	270.3	33.4	966.5
1984	44.0	61.9	334.1	49.9	152.5	264.8	31.6	938.8

1985	42.0	59.1	302.6	47.2	a	259.4	31.3	892.4
1986	41.0	55.9	273.5	42.8		251.3	29.9	837.0
1987	42.0	54.9	268.4	39.8	133.3		28.5	799.2
1988	40.7	55.1	277.2	38.6	131.1	206.9		777.5
1989	39.5	53.8	274.3	37.6	130.5	198.8	2.	762.1
1990	32.3	52.6	270.2	36.9	127.0	194.5	26.6	
1970-1990								
Absolute change	−15.2	−169.8	−279.4	−45.7	−110.7	−150.7	−14.4	−785.9
Percentage change	−32.0	−76.3	−50.8	−55.3	−46.6	−43.7	−35.1	−51.5

SOURCE: OECD printout, Paris, 1991.

a=six countries.

n.a.=not available.

excess capacity with corresponding workforce reduction (McKersie and Sengenberger 1981). This form of restructuring can be distinguished from external restructuring, which is related to the decline of some industries and firms and the growth of others and is often accompanied by a reallocation of capital and labor (Bluestone and Harrison 1982). The distinction between these two can be blurred if adjustment comes about, as it has in steel, through mergers of firms, product diversification and other forms of industry reorganization.

The typology used in this book (see figure 1.2) permits cross-national comparisons. This typology relies on the work of Bamber and Lansbury (1987), Katzenstein (1985), Lipset (1986), and Ulman (1987). The eight industrialized countries are divided into two types of industrial relations systems: adversarial and cooperative. The adversarial systems are Canada, Great Britain, and the United States. Unions and employers in these countries have negotiated at arms length from one another. Individual demands are framed away from the table, and there is a minimum of communication. Government has generally not intervened in economic activity, but has allowed the market to dictate the outcomes. Worker participation is through collective bargaining, which takes place most often at the company level. Income security programs are negotiated with little government assistance. These countries exhibit the "monopoly" face of unions (Freeman and Medoff 1984). The bargaining process and outcomes are based on the position that unions increase costs and reduce productivity growth. Unions are expected to reallocate resources toward labor and away from restructuring and competitive resources.

The cooperative systems examined in this study are Belgium, Germany, Japan, Luxembourg, and Sweden. These countries exhibit a social partnership where information is shared and there is joint problemsolving. Government has intervened in industrial policy with substantial and continuous financial assistance. Worker participation is through collective bargaining, works councils, and consultation at the national, regional, and shop-floor levels. These countries exhibit the "voice" face of unions (Freeman and Medoff 1984). The bargaining process and outcomes are based on the position that unions enhance productivity by reducing turnover which in turn increases employees' knowledge of the specific jobs they perform.

Figure 1.1
The Determinants of Restructuring
A Conceptual Framework

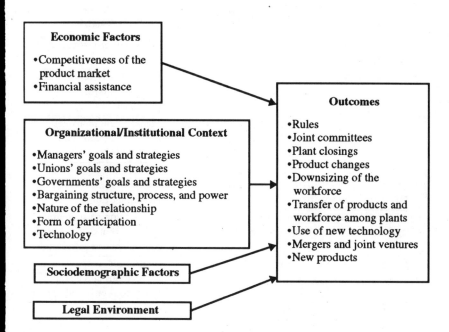

Economic Factors

- Competitiveness of the product market
- Financial assistance

Organizational/Institutional Context

- Managers' goals and strategies
- Unions' goals and strategies
- Governments' goals and strategies
- Bargaining structure, process, and power
- Nature of the relationship
- Form of participation
- Technology

Sociodemographic Factors

Legal Environment

Outcomes

- Rules
- Joint committees
- Plant closings
- Product changes
- Downsizing of the workforce
- Transfer of products and workforce among plants
- Use of new technology
- Mergers and joint ventures
- New products

Figure 1.2
Comparative Industrial Relations Systems Matrix

Environmental issues	Adversarial countries (Canada, Great Britain, United States)	Cooperative countries (Belgium, Germany, Japan, Luxembourg, Sweden)
Competitiveness of the product market	Laissez-faire	Interventionist, some central planning
Financial assistance	Private and internal	External government loans or grants and private assistance
Managers' goals and strategies	Management innovates	Management innovates with joint participation and consultation
Unions' goals and strategies	Economic and focused on individual members	Economic and political focused on membership and firm organization
Governments' goals and strategies	Laissez-faire and noninterventionist	Interventionist; sometimes full or partial ownership of firms and some laissez-faire
Bargaining structure	Decentralized	Centralized; employers associations and union federations or by enterprise
Nature of the relationship	Adversarial	Cooperative
Form of participation	Collective bargaining and negotiations; limits on worker participation	Codetermination; and quality circles
Technology	Dependent on management and some negotiation	Employee participation
Sociodemographic factors	Middle-aged, male	Middle-aged, male
Legal environment	Not directly related to restructuring; law regulates health, safety, and the environment	Legislation directly concerned with restructuring and rationalization. Plant-closing legislation and government-sponsored studies of impact on communities

There is some difficulty in generalizing the characteristics of the eight countries into two broad categories, particularly for Germany and Japan, since they possess characteristics of both the adversarial and cooperative systems.

In assessing labor's role in the adjustment process, it is necessary to determine whether different systems have different effects on restructuring. However, it is important to move beyond describing union-management relations in restructuring to assessing the impact of alternative approaches to adjustment. This study attempts to provide answers to the following questions.

1. What were the differences in the adjustment process between the two types of industrial relations systems?

2. Which approach was more efficient from the point of view of labor and society?

3. Who bore the costs of adjustment?

The methodology used in this book is inductive and employs case study analysis. Beginning in 1982, more then 100 interviews were conducted with managers, union officials, and works council representatives in the steel industry in the eight countries. These interviews were supplemented by interviews with government officials and academicians. Preliminary findings were shared with the parties in the eight countries. Data reported are from national and local union contracts, works council records, company reports, the Commission of the European Communities (CEC), the Organization for Economic Cooperation and Development (OECD), and the U.S. State Department.

The book is organized in matrix form. The environmental issues presented in figure 1.2 are examined across the eight countries. Belgium and Luxembourg are discussed together because their restructuring plans became interdependent.

Chapter 2 examines the environmental factors that affected restructuring. It illustrates the cross-national differences in the role of government between the adversarial and cooperative countries. Government played a minor role in restructuring in the adversarial countries, except in Great Britain. It played a much more central role in the cooperative countries.

Chapter 3 describes union-management negotiations in the adversarial countries. In these countries, the unions focused on the bargaining table. Plants were closed, and in two companies there were lengthy and pervasive strikes.

Chapter 4 describes union-management negotiations as well as other forms of employee participation in the cooperative countries. Plants often closed gradually, and workers were transferred; where strikes occurred, they were short. Employee participation in decision-making also cushioned the impact on the workers.

Chapter 5 presents the results of negotiations over income security. This chapter demonstrates that in adversarial countries, the employees and their companies bore the greatest costs of restructuring, while in cooperative countries government bore the major cost.

Chapter 6 offers conclusions.

2
Restructuring in Eight Countries

This chapter describes how restructuring took place in the eight countries, and includes the role of the European Economic Community (EEC) as well as that of the various governments. The determinants presented in figure 1.1 influenced the outcomes. It can be hypothesized that adversarial countries would restructure using private resources, with little interference or assistance from government. Cooperative countries, on the other hand, could be expected to restructure with considerable government assistance, through planning, loans, or government ownership.

The basic steel industry is composed of three types of firms: integrated, specialty, and mini-mills. This book concentrates on integrated firms. Using the oxygen method, the integrated firm smelts raw materials such as iron ore and coal in blast furnaces and then refines the metal into steel in oxygen converters. The final products are primarily flat rolled steel, such as plate or hot and cold rolled sheet. Traditionally, only mills using the oxygen method have been capable of large-scale production; however, this distinction has been blurred in recent years as mini-mills have experienced a significant increase in size and production capacity. Figure 2.1 compares the production process of the integrated mill with the mini-mill.

Integrated steelworks are large and are among the biggest capital investments found on a single site in any industry. The technical characteristics of steelmaking give rise to marked economies of scale (Aylen 1982). There are major cost advantages to building large plants, providing they are fully utilized. There is also a large fixed-cost element in steelwork operations arising from supervision and materials handling. Manning levels hardly increase as the throughput of a plant rises. There is, therefore, a wide gap between total costs and variable costs because of high capital intensity and a chronic tendency to develop surplus capacity. Economics of scale were reinforced by innovations, such as the basic oxygen furnace (BOF) and continuous casting, during the 1960s and 1970s.

14

Figure 2.1
The Steelmaking Process

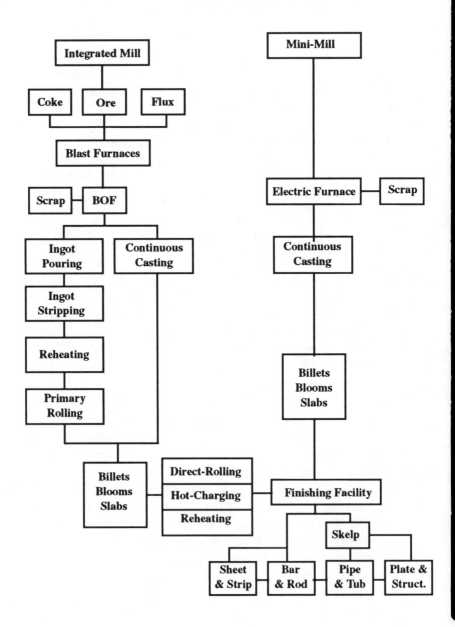

These integrated steelworks affect the physical environment because of their size, requirements for transportation, ore and coke yards, high-production facilities, and cooling tanks. Their influence is not confined to the principal environment. They also affect the region's economic structure, since they are often the area's largest employer (Hoerr 1988; Schroter 1986; Bradbury 1987). Other industries may be repelled, and medium and small firms are discouraged from locating in the area, since steel wages are higher than those of other firms competing for the same employees. Layoffs under these conditions are a burden to workers and their families in a community that has few sources of alternative employment (Buss and Redburn 1983).

Adversarial Systems

Canada

Canadian steel underwent the least restructuring of any of the eight countries in this study, and it was one of the two countries to increase its production, Japan being the other (Barnett and Schorsch 1983; Bradbury 1987). Production increased by 9.64 percent (see table 1.1) while employment was reduced by 32 percent (see table 1.2). The four integrated iron and steel producers in Canada are Dofasco, which merged with Algoma in 1988, and Stelco, both private firms, and two smaller publicly owned companies, Sidbec-Dosco and Sydney Steel. The privately owned firms have supplied about 80 percent of the industry's output during the past 25 years and have been consistently profitable. The two publicly owned companies, however, have had problems because of a heavy debt structure involving large interest payments. They incurred substantial losses, which resulted in government subsidies from both the federal and provincial governments.

The Canadian steel industry has managed to become one of the most profitable in the world, despite the limitations of a small domestic market and the importance of size for economies of scale. The strategic elements leading to this success are a high degree of product specialization to achieve economies of scale and international cost competitiveness, and minimization of interfirm rivalries by virtue of specialization. High operating rates have also been maintained by bringing in sufficient productive capacity only for markets in which a comparative advantage could be realized by taking into account transport costs and tariffs. The Canadian steel industry also has the advantage of supplying the U.S.-owned auto industry. Twenty percent of its steel has gone to autos (Algoma Steel 1983). The efficient use of energy and power—perhaps half that of the United States and a third that of Japan—has also contributed to the success of Canadian steel. Excess demand and/or unprofitable markets have been serviced through imports. In times of economic downturn, some of the unprofitable geographic and product markets have been serviced by the domestic steel producers. New technologies for products and processes have been quickly adopted, largely from foreign sources. Dofasco was the first company to introduce BOF steelmaking and continuous casting in North America.

Canadian steel prepared itself well for increased competition in the 1980s. The integrated firms made good management decisions regarding capital investment, as well as operating and sales practices. They were successful, despite the fact that they had no particular advantages in terms of raw materials. Virtually all of their coal comes from the United States at a price equal to and in some instances slightly higher than that paid by the U.S. steel industry. A significant portion of ore is imported, although ore is also obtained from domestic sources. The industry has concentrated on the domestic market.

In 1982, Stelco built a greenfield site integrated plant in Hamilton with a blast furnace, two oxygen converters, a continuous caster and a continuous hot-strip mill. Dofasco in the same year, constructed a second hot-strip mill and Algoma constructed a seamless-pipe mill.

The worldwide decline in steel demand in 1982 and 1983 also resulted in a drop in production, a general loss of revenue, and a 23 percent decline in steel employment in Canada. However, the steel companies and workers were not subject to the same pressures that existed for the United States, European, and Japanese steel companies, since Canadian steel producers hadn't engaged in the cycle of first building overcapacity and then restructuring that occurred in the United States and Europe.

Great Britain

Steel in Great Britain underwent more changes than in any other country in this study, with large-scale reductions in the labor force and massive plant closings. Production was reduced by 36.75 percent (see table 1.1), and three out of four jobs were eliminated (see table 1.2). At the same time, the government-owned British Steel Corporation (BSC) engaged in extensive and tenacious negotiations with the trade unions. These negotiations are discussed in chapter 3.

By the 1960s, steel had come to occupy a very unique place in British party politics, signifying perhaps more than anything else the policy distance between the Conservative and Labor parties (Ovenden 1978). With the nationalization of the 14 largest companies into the BSC in 1967, the adversarial approach had declined, and by the early 1970s, consensus politics had emerged. The BSC became a vital symbol of both parties' intent to foster general industrial growth.

British steel policy and its implementation were highly dependent on an alliance between BSC and the government which was not always smooth. Management at BSC and the government often disagreed on policy. Although the BSC was accountable to a cabinet minister and Parliament, the power balance of the relationship, in reality, tilted in favor of the top management of the BSC with its specialized expertise, which was challenged only occasionally by the government (Richardson and Duley 1986). At the same time, large sums of public money were necessary for the purpose of restructuring. The BSC faced several crises in the 1970s. The Ten-Year Program of 1973, developed by the Conservative government, called for building a capacity of 38 million tons (Bryer, Brignall, and Maunders 1982). This target was questioned immediately because of the 1973-1974 oil crisis and a decline in demand from autos, shipbuilding, and construction. The plants that BSC had inherited from the private sector also had outdated technology and a large workforce. A 1970 development plan envisioned production of more than 40 million tons *per annum* by 1980, with the construction of major new greenfield works at Redcar and production at five large coastal works: Ravenscraig, Tesside, Scunthorpe, Llanwern, and Port Talbot. This plan was modified by a government task force which reduced projected capacity to 28 to 30 million tons. This strategy was expected to result in the loss of an additional 30,000 jobs on top of the 20,000-job loss anticipated by an earlier strategy. The Conservative government gave relatively few details of the plants to be closed, preferring to take the political approach by giving the BSC the responsibility for announcing plant closings.

The return of the Labor party to power in 1974 required the new government to resolve its conflict between economic reality and jobs. The issue was how to reduce capacity while protecting the interests of steelworkers, who represented one of its largest constituencies. While the government debated a plan of slow change, the BSC launched its own plan involving the closure of unprofitable steelworks, the concentration of production in plants with modern technology, a reduction in manpower, an attempt to increase the company's local business identity, a reduction in central control and managerial overhead, and an improvement in direct communications with the workforce. Direct communications became part of a social policy aimed at softening the effects of change and creating a climate where change would become more acceptable. The social policy included a consultation process involving employees, trade unions, and local government; counseling programs for individual employees; voluntary quit arrangements; early retirement; retraining; compensation payments for leaving the corporation; and job creation programs.

In 1977, BSC had 23 steelmaking centers. Many of these centers relied on outdated technology and work practices that inhibited productivity growth. Continued operation of these plants increased the risk of the Corporation collapsing, and BSC decided to close down all costly operations. During the same year, the Labor government abandoned its noninterventionist approach when it realized that BSC's financial position was deteriorating. It accepted plant closings while encouraging BSC to offer large severance payments to laid-off employees. The Labor government supported this approach by increasing the BSC's borrowing limit in response to escalating losses ($234 million in 1979-80).[1]

The immense significance of the three-month steel strike at the beginning of 1980 is discussed in chapter 3.

In June 1980, Ian MacGregor was appointed chairman of BSC under a Conservative government, and downsizing continued. The company polled its employees on a plan to eliminate 20,000 jobs, and although the unions hotly disputed this plan, the majority of the workforce accepted it. The issue was preserving some jobs or none.

The Conservative government was anxious to privatize BSC, and the company was split into a number of profit centers, taking management decisions away from the head office and giving them to local management. The new structure was based on product specialization, and separate companies were started at the same time that capacity was reduced by cutting back on the number of blast furnaces and melting shops. BSC also sold its non-steel-related affiliates and ended a number of joint ventures.

Restructuring brought large increases in labor productivity, despite a severe drop in output. Man-hours needed to make a ton of steel at BSC were more than halved between the 1980/81 and 1983/84 financial years. Labor productivity at the Llanwern works increased six times between 1975 and 1984, and Port Talbot also achieved world standards for productivity levels.

BSC began to emerge by the mid-1980s as a profitable maker of steel and increased production back up to 14.7 million tons. The British government had forgiven most of the loans to the company. BSC continued to cut employment, which fell to 53,000 in 1988. By improving manufacturing methods and cutting employment, the company made a large improvement in productivity and reduced the number of man-hours to produce a ton of steel from 14.5 in 1980 to 5 in 1988. As of November 1988, British Steel had spent $435, before taxes, per ton of steel shipped, compared to industry averages of $445 in France, $467 in West Germany, $475 in the United States, and $535 in Japan. The reader should be warned that cross-country comparisons of the cost of steelmaking vary from year-to-year and country-to-country with changes in exchange rates (*Wall Street Journal*, November 16, 1988).

BSC showed a profit of $672 million in 1987 after 10 years of deficits (*Economist*, October 29, 1988). This turnaround was capped by the British government's privatization of the company in November 1988.

United States

The United States was second only to Great Britain in the relative size of the changes in its steel industry, which declined by 25 percent between 1970 and 1990 (see table 1.1) and lost half of its jobs (see table 1.2).[2] The major structural changes in steel began during the recession of 1982 in response to the problems of overcapacity and the influx of foreign steel products. Imports entered the domestic market during a 116-day strike in 1959 when customers turned to overseas steel manufacturers (Goldberg 1986). This import trend continued, with substantial increases every three years as customers sought a hedge against the impact of a possible strike. In 1975, there were 20 integrated steel companies with 47 operating plants in the United States, but by 1987, the number of companies had been reduced to 14 with 23 plants. These changes were accomplished by the retirement of older, inefficient plants and equipment, a change in pricing policy from base point plus shipping costs pricing to competitive pricing, mergers, joint ventures, diversification, and divestiture. New labor agreements also provided for wage and work practice concessions. This is discussed in chapter 3.

Most companies used at least one of these strategies, which resulted in large reductions in employment. The abandonment of submarginal facilities by multiplant firms had a significant impact particularly in the historic steelmaking region stretching from Pittsburgh to Youngstown (Fuechtmann 1989; Hoerr 1988). One author maintained that closings in 1977-1979 were "helter-skelter," and that more gradual phasing out of the facilities would have made it possible to transfer some of the surplus workers to other operations in order to hold down the enormous separation costs that rise from dismissal. Unprofitable product lines and their relevant facilities in surviving plants and firms were closed. This trend clearly established more specialization among the largest firms.

In a well-designed merger, a steel firm might achieve profitability. It becomes much easier to close high-cost facilities without leaving a market segment. Large capital outlays may not be necessary, as assets are combined and selling and administrative costs are reduced with one group of managers instead of two. In 1984, the Youngstown Sheet and Tube Corporation was acquired by the Jones and Laughlin Corporation, which was owned by Ling-Temco-Vought (LTV). Subsequently, Jones and Laughlin merged with Republic Steel Corporation under LTV, forming the nation's second largest steel producer. The merger was approved by the Justice Department after an original rejection and considerable controversy. The reason given for the initial rejection was that it would have created a firm with too large a share of the flat-rolled steel market. The key reason for the about-face by government was the agreement by the two firms to sell two Republic plants, a flat-rolled mill in Gadsden, Alabama and a stainless steel sheet finishing facility in Massillon, Ohio. This action cut the resulting market share to an acceptable level. The Justice Department's actions served notice of the existence of a maximum market share of approximately 20 percent, the amount resulting from the amended LTV merger, that could be held by any one steelmaker in the flat-rolled steel market. The Justice Department also required LTV to retain all pension and debt liabilities at Gadsden and Massillon for 10 years. To prevent possible price collusion, the Department prohibited LTV from supplying operating data to the American Iron & Steel Institute for a period of 10 years.

Joint ventures were also undertaken by the U.S. firms. This strategy is most applicable at a greenfield site where joint ownership can be established at the outset. Joint ventures involve mutual division of ownership as well as mutual location decisions. In a highly capital-intensive industry where capital funds are scarce, a joint venture offers the advantages of reducing each firm's contribution and reducing unit costs because of higher utilization rates. Bethlehem and Inland Steel joined in a venture to produce electro galvanized steel, and USS joined with Pohan of South Korea and Worthington Industries of the United States.

A number of foreign producers have also invested in the domestic steel industry. Nippon Kokan acquired 50 percent of National Steel's steel subsidiary in 1984 and another 40 percent in 1990. In 1984, Kaiser Steel sold its Fontana, California plant to a joint venture among Californian, Brazilian and Japanese companies.

Diversification is another strategy by which many integrated producers have sought to give some sense of balance to their income statements. By entering into new businesses, the downside of the steel cycle can be somewhat offset and overall corporate profit levels smoothed. Good examples are National Steel's acquisition of United Financial of California and two other banks and the purchase by United States Steel (USS) of Marathon Oil. After failing in its effort to acquire National Steel, USS proceeded to spend more than one-half billion dollars to buy Canada's Husky Oil Company. With its $3 billion purchase of

Texas Oil & Gas in 1983, USS appeared to be following a clear path of disinvestment in steel, including a renaming of the company to USX. USS was kept as the name of the steel division. David Roderick, USX chairman, when explaining the rationale for the oil investment, declared, "U.S. Steel . . . will invest our cash flow where we can make money. If that leads to further diversification, so be it." With regard to divestiture, many firms, in an effort to generate funds for technological improvements, have been forced to evaluate the composition of the asset side of their respective corporate balance sheets. Raw material reserves and unneeded equipment have been the primary items discarded for cash. This move has been an important part of the steel industry's strategy, since cash for technological upgrading is one of the highest priorities in the industry. The sale of National Steel's Weirton plant to its employees in 1983-84 avoided shutdown costs and allowed National to continue in steel (Torrence 1989).

USS provides a case study of the typical structural changes that took place among the integrated firms. USS had long been the industry leader, but the company experienced adversity during the late 1970s and early 1980s. Capital shortages produced imbalances among stages of the production process, and new foreign and domestic competitive forces caused USS to undergo massive changes between 1977 and 1984 and embark on a new strategy toward its steel operations.

USS, like other integrated steel producers, decided to make drastic changes in technology in its steel facilities in the mid-1970s. At the beginning of the 1970s, USS had intended to upgrade both hot-end and finishing-end equipment at many facilities, and many USS facilities were in the middle of modernization when the steel market began to decline. As the market declined, most modernization projects were discontinued, which left their mills with severe imbalances in technology. Some phases of the process had been modernized and others had not. USS decided to develop only four facilities: Fairfield, Alabama; Lorain, Ohio; Gary, Indiana; and Baytown, Texas. At Fairfield in 1986, following a union agreement to change restrictive work rules and to withdraw manning grievances, USS began the construction of a $750 million seamless-pipe mill and continuous bloom caster. The agreement will be discussed in chapter 3. In 1983, after the reopening of the Fairfield facility, which had been closed since June of 1982, USS announced plans to build a $200 million dollar continuous slab caster at Fairfield Works and improve the hot-strip facility and the cold-reduction mill. This upgrade was completed in 1989.

In 1981, USS announced that a new continuous round caster would also be built in Lorain. This equipment was meant to reduce energy use by 50 percent because of the elimination of ingot pouring, stripping, and rolling, and was a part of a $145 million modernization plan at Lorain. Also included was computerized process control equipment designed to optimize BOF-to-caster performance. This caster was designed to work in tandem with the preexisting pipe facilities at Lorain. In 1984, modifications were made to the round caster to enable it to also produce billets, the basis of rod- and wire-related products. Rod operations, which were curtailed with closings at other facilities, were moved to Lorain for modern, low-cost production.

In 1982, the old Gary Works slab caster, USS's first, was modernized, and funds were approved for the construction of a second caster to provide more durable slab for hot-strip facilities.

USS has also sought to diversify into other lines of business, divest itself of unprofitable or unneeded assets, and enter into joint ventures with other producers. It began in 1980 to sell off assets, which included its large Universal Atlas Cement Company, its corporate headquarters in Pittsburgh, an electrical cord division, and a tire cord division. Universal Atlas was sold to a German firm, primarily because its continued profitability would have required extensive capital infusions which USS was unprepared to make. The sell-offs also included raw material reserves. In the late 1970s, USS sold some 49,000 acres of timberland to International Paper and further timber assets to the Mead Corporation. Conoco entered into an agreement to lease USS coal properties, and Soqui agreed to purchase three coal mines and one-fourth of the company's coal reserves. At one time, it was estimated that USS owned enough unneeded coal reserves to last 100 years at full operational levels.

Restructuring produced results: by 1985, man-hours per ton of steel produced had been reduced at USS from 10.18 to 6. In addition, break-even utilization rates were reduced from 80 percent to 60 percent in 1981. During one quarter in 1989, USS realized more income from its steel operations than it had in the previous 10 years. USS's policies for its steel division only partially mirror the rest of the industry. USS diversified more than the other firms, particularly into energy, and at this writing there are indications that it may sell its steel division. Other U.S. firms, such as Bethlehem and LTV, have taken the opposite approach and concentrated on their core steel business.

Cooperative Systems

Belgium and Luxembourg

Belgium and Luxembourg are discussed together in this book because their steel industries are connected through joint ownership and joint restructuring. Steel production in these two countries declined by 17 percent between 1970 and 1990 (see table 1.1) and half the jobs were eliminated (see table 1.2).

Steel restructuring in Belgium has two characteristics: the rivalry between the older steel-producing Wallonia region in the south and the newer steel-producing Flemish region in the north, and the very strong participation of the central government. State intervention in steel moved between 1977 and 1981 from tripartite participation among government, the trade unions, and the steel employers association, to financial support without control, to a share in the steel firms, and finally to a government takeover of Cockerill-Sambre. The government first assisted, then became a partial owner, and finally initiated the major restructuring plan.[3]

Belgium expanded capacity between 1968 and 1975 and switched to oxygen steel production during that time. The most marked technological developments were in the continuous annealing of sheet, in the treating of the surface of sheet, particularly the coating by organic and inorganic products and the ever-increasing computerization of the production process, with a view to improving the quality of products.

The feud between Wallonia and Flanders was accentuated by the creation of the Sidmar complex near Ghent in the north in 1961 and dramatized by a strike in May-June 1977 at the Chertal site owned by Cockerill, a southern company, against what was perceived as a planned increase in capacity at Sidmar. Arbed and the Luxembourg government were majority owners of Sidmar, and each region asserted that assistance to one steel firm had to be matched by compensation to the other. Between 1976 and 1980, Wallonia received $2.65 billion for steel assistance, while Flanders received $5.61 million. This difference was offset by aid to Flanders for its coal, shipbuilding and textile industries. Government aid for Cockerill-Sambre was also viewed by the north as threatening the extension of the Flemish steel sector and restricting financial aid that would be available to other Flemish industries, such as textiles. Eventually, a financial limit was set on the central government's contribution to Cockerill-Sambre. Above this limit the Wallonia region would be responsible for funding within the framework of the national budget. A government share in the steel firms was gradually acquired during 1979. By the end of that year, the government controlled 28.9 percent of Cockerill, a national planning committee was created to approve and direct steel investment, and a series of plant studies were undertaken to ensure the survival of Cockerill-Sambre.

The question of industrial policy and the threat of rupture between Flanders and Wallonia were the major issues. The difficulties of Cockerill-Sambre became a test case for the political and institutional future of Belgium. The holding companies in steel sought to get the government to assume a greater part of the risk without relinquishing their decisionmaking powers. The steel industry in Belgium, particularly Cockerill-Sambre, suffered from reduced sales for much of the 1970s and into the 1980s and had to reduce employment. While Cockerill-Sambre's economic strength ebbed, Sidmar, with a modern integrated facility, remained healthy. Cockerill-Sambre reduced employment by 50 percent between 1974 and 1983, while Sidmar increased its employment by 24 percent during the same period.[4] In 1974, Cockerill-Sambre accounted for 62 percent and Sidmar 14 percent of total steel employment in Belgium. However, by 1983, this gap had been narrowed to 47 percent and 28 percent, respectively.

Important for the maintenance of government assistance to Cockerill-Sambre were the political ties between the socialist General Belgium Labor Federation and the socialist Belgium government. The Metal Workers is one of the strongest of unions in the Labor Federation. The central government received strong support from the socialist Metal Workers Union, and assisted Cockerill-Sambre. Tripartite agreements between the government, unions, and companies resulted in central government aid for modernization and the repayment of Cockerill-

Sambre's debt. The employment implications of this agreement are discussed in chapter 5. In 1980, a system was installed called "advanced recuperable funds." Cockerill-Sambre was able to borrow money using a government guarantee for its loans, while the government handled Cockerill-Sambre's payments. After five years, the company, was to reimburse the government. However, because of the continued decline of the company, this assistance continued after 1985.

A shift in the government took place in December 1981 from the socialists to a Catholic-liberal coalition. This coalition had considerable voter strength in the north, and the new government sought to change the state's role in assisting Cockerill-Sambre. At the same time the EEC set quotas and mandated restructuring for steel production. The EEC's role in restructuring is discussed at the end of this chapter. In order to meet EEC's requirements, a plan for revitalizing the steel industry was developed in 1984 called the Gandois Plan, after Jean Gandois, a French steel expert hired by the Belgium government to examine Cockerill-Sambre and by the Luxembourg government to study Arbed. First, an agreement to share restructuring was sought with the Netherlands. When this fell through, the Gandois Plan anticipated meeting the EEC quotas by combining steel facilities in Belgium and Luxembourg. The Gandois Plan integrated the steel in the two countries. Maximum rolled steel output was set, the number of steel forges reduced from four to two, cold-rolling mills were reduced from five to four, semifinished products were transferred between Liege and Charleroi, and external supplies were arranged through international production agreements. In September 1983, the Belgium government acquired 22 percent of Arbed, the Luxembourg steel firm, by subscribing to an Arbed loan. Several older plants in Charleroi, Liege, and Luxembourg were slated to be closed, including Liege's modern Valfil steel wire rod mill, in favor of an Arbed plant in Schifflange, and quotas were to be assigned to enable Cockerill-Sambre and Arbed to meet EEC limitations. At the same time, Arbed would close its hot-strip mill in Dudelange in 1985 and transfer its production to Cockerill-Sambre's Carlam works. Plant closings were traded for the avoidance of layoffs. Plant closings were expected to eliminate 1,000 jobs in Belgium in the near term and eventually between 7,900 and 9,000 jobs in Cockerill-Sambre between 1983 and 1985. Layoffs were to be avoided, with reductions coming by early retirements, attrition, and transfers.

Employment policy is discussed in chapter 5. A 1984 plan further integrated steel in the two countries.

Arbed restructured in 1984, the Luxembourg government increased its share in the company to 24.5 percent, and the major banks provided rolling loans (Hargreaves 1984). Arbed and Cockerill-Sambre agreed to cooperate in the establishment of product specialization. Arbed's Luxembourg Works were to specialize in nonflat rolled products, Sidmar in hot- and cold-rolled flat products, Liege in cold-rolled and coated flat, and Chaleroi in hot-rolled flat.

The new central government in Belgium also sought to limit its involvement in bailing out the Wallonia-based Cockerill-Sambre by fixing the amount given to the company at $155 million for early pensions and $52 million for economic development. An ending date of 1985 was set for the central government assistance. After that date, the burden was to be shifted to the southern regional government, and all future financing for Cockerill-Sambre was to come from the Wallonia regional government's revenues augmented by its share of the inheritance taxes collected by the central government. The restructuring plan was presented to the trade unions in the hope of getting their support before submitting it to a referendum of the workforce; however, the unions resisted and the plan was dropped.

The key aspects of Belgium restructuring were the issue of equal treatment for northern and southern steel and the role of the EEC, discussed at the end of this chapter. The leverage that the EEC used was the loss or suspension of a loan for specific investments in Belgium steel.

The steel industry in Luxembourg was more dominant in that country's economy than steel in any of the other countries in this study. About one-third of the workforce had been employed in iron and steel production, the highest proportion among all European countries. The rapid decline in the industry's workforce, by more than 50 percent between 1976 and 1982, and the difficulty in providing the workers with alternative employment encouraged cooperation between Arbed, the trade unions, and the government. The Steel Tripartite Commission adopted a restructuring agreement in 1979 (Schneider 1980). The parties set up an Anticrisis Division for Arbed and a smaller firm, which had the task of finding new jobs for redundant steelworkers. A tight network of labor-management information and consultation was established by the parties to work out joint solutions to the problems of restructuring. The Anticrisis Division will be discussed in chapter 5. There was close cooperation between the public authorities, the steel companies, and the trade unions in attempts to attract investment for the creation of employment. Collective agreements provided for various forms of financial assistance, which supplemented state unemployment benefits and benefits granted under an agreement between the government and the EEC. Tight government controls were introduced to curtail overtime and restrict the employment of persons who had reached the age of retirement.

Germany

German steel production declined by 15 percent from 1979-90 (see table 1.1) and eliminated almost half of its jobs (see table 1.2). Restructuring was a combination of public and private efforts, with strong union opposition to plant closings. Federal and state government support was concentrated in the Saar (Goldberg 1986).

In 1970, half of the value of the Saar's production was in raw and rolled steel, and it was this dependency on steel that forced the government to bolster the industry in the hope of avoiding a regional decline. However, the Saar was disadvantaged. Its location was poor, it depended on ore and oil imports, and it had access only to high-cost local coal. Steel consisted of a large number of small to medium-sized, often family-owned, plants, with no steel-using customers downstream. In 1976 and 1977, the state and federal governments guaranteed loans of $69 million to keep Neukirchen Eisenwerke (NE) open. When NE and Rochling Burbach threatened to shut down their Saar plants, the state found a buyer in Arbed, and the government and the unions accepted Arbed's plans for restructuring the facilities and the workforce. The new firm, Arbed Saarstahl, used the same labor market programs in the Saar as it had employed in Luxembourg. These are discussed in chapter 5.

The federal and state government continued to support the Saar as it suffered a 23 percent job loss in steel between 1977 and 1978. Federal labor programs provided funds for regions with special labor problems. Companies could claim funds to retain the unskilled and long-term unemployed and to set up new jobs in the social services. Most of the money was used in the Saar, with 83 percent being used for retraining between 1979-1980. In spite of slashing crude steel production by 37 percent from 1977 to 1982, the Saar remained in trouble. It was bailed out by state funds in 1982 and 1983, but was still in trouble in 1984 when steel in the Ruhr also encountered difficulties.

Production of German steel was concentrated in seven companies which produced 94.1 percent of all crude steel in 1979 and 33 percent of the EEC's crude and rolled steel (Esser and Vath 1986). The largest center of steel production was in the Ruhr with Thyssen, Krupp, Hoesch and Klockner. While most of the European countries were building new plants on the coast, which would give them access to overseas ore and coal, German companies chose to modernize the best of the existing plants in the Rhine and Ruhr regions.

German firms have restructured in the same manner as those in the United States, through mergers and diversification. Hoesch joined with Hoogovens and Thyssen with Rheinstahl. Krupp, Mannesmann, and Thyssen developed into conglomerates. Krupp reduced its emphasis on steel and moved into industrial construction and turnkey projects. Mannesmann moved into machinery, and Thyssen into heavy goods and industrial construction. For Thyssen, losses in steel of $160 million were covered by gains in other sectors.

The government's role is illustrated by the cases of Hoesch and Krupp in 1981. When Hoesch sought help in restructuring its debt of $1.6 billion and Krupp asked for a loan guarantee, the government suggested the merger of the two companies into Ruhrstahl. The companies came up with a plan for restructuring production and reducing labor in October 1981. The government sought to assist the companies though the creation of a program of job replacement at steel sites, transition projects for employees over the age of 50, extension of the research program for steel, and an investment grant over three years for restructuring and modernizing. This plan for a new, larger firm was blocked by the unions.

In January 1983, proposals for restructuring were presented by a group of independent experts and included marketing proposals and a regrouping of the steel industry into a Rhine Group (Thyssen and Krupp) and a Ruhr Group (Hoesch, Peine-Salzgitter, Klockner-Maxhutte). Germany was the last member of the EEC to resort to a government bailout of its steel industry and was reluctant to agree to EEC quotas on steel production. Germany viewed steel firms in the other EEC countries as responsible for the crisis by failing to restructure and by allowing nationalized firms that were not profitable to be kept open with public subsidies. Criticism centered not on the aid for displaced workers, but on retention of capacity. In return for reducing their objectives, firms achieved concessions under the EEC quota system. The EEC quota system will be discussed in the last section of this chapter.

When the German cabinet finally approved a restructuring plan in June 1983, it authorized $1.17 billion in government subsidies to help German steel companies cover the $4.28 billion in costs for restructuring and the slashing of capacity to 13 million metric tons. Half of the subsidies would be paid by the central government and half by the state governments. Three groups were proposed: Rhine (Thyssen and Krupp), Ruhr (Hoesch and Peine), and Klockner. Before the plan was ever approved, however, the Ruhr Group fell apart. Krupp-Stahl AG was in receivership and was not included in the plan.

Restructuring faced another setback when plans for merging Thyssen and Krupp dissolved at the end of 1984. Krupp had another merger planned with Klockner and CRA Ltd. of Australia which would have created one of West Germany's largest steel companies (*Wall Street Journal,* October 25, 1984). Krupp and Klockner hoped to save $89 million (in 1984 U.S. dollars) annually from these mergers. Because the merger would result in the closure of a mill and the loss of 1,200 jobs in the state of Lower Saxony, the unions and Lower Saxony vehemently opposed the merger. The merger ultimately failed when Lower Saxony refused to pay its one-third share of the $250 million the companies wanted in government subsidies to cover costs of restructuring.[5]

Despite the failures to restructure, German steel continued to prosper, and the large firms modernized while holding down costs and prices at the same time that they were diversifying. However, lean times began again in 1986 because of the weaker American dollar, U.S. steel import restrictions, imports of less expensive non-European steel, and increased government subsidies to the steel industry in other EEC countries. Further cuts were made in steel production and employment, and the federal government took further steps to help its ailing steel industry by excusing Arbed Saarstahl from repaying $335 million of the $850 million it had received. The Saarland government also waived

$238 million it was owed by Arbed Saarstahl. Once the company was debt free, the government planned to buy a 76 percent share and then sell part of its holdings to Dillinger, a French firm who would assume management control. This was accomplished. Since 1978, Saarstahl had received $1.25 billion in government subsidies (*Economist*, March 29, 1986). In October 1987, the West German government also announced a $333 million aid plan to help the 35,000 workers scheduled to be eliminated from the steel industry by 1989. The costs of the program were to be shared by the federal government, the steel producing states and the EEC. Steelmakers, such as Thyssen, planned to contribute close to $666 million in additional aid to the workers (*Wall Street Journal*, October 6, 1987).

In November 1987, another attempt to restructure part of Germany's steel industry was proposed as Thyssen, Mannesmann, and Krupp announced a plan to cut costs by merging parts of their operations in the Ruhr valley. The three companies hoped to save money, reduce overcapacity, and comply with EEC demands for output reductions (*Wall Street Journal*, November 27, 1987). The plan called for the closing of Krupp's plant at Rheinhausen, but when the plant workers heard of the plan, they held some of the angriest demonstrations in decades, blocking roads and bridges in the Ruhr (*Economist*, January 23, 1988). Krupp was forced to modify its position. It still planned to close the Rheinhausen mill, but it proposed creating substitute jobs or giving early pensions to all but 1,300 of the affected workers (*Wall Street Journal*, January 28, 1988). A social plan for Krupp was worked out with the cooperation of Mannesmann and Thyssen. These companies pledged to hire some of the Krupp workers, and the phase-out continued until the end of the 1990.

Restructuring after 1975 was characterized by a distinction between the severely disadvantaged Saar, which required massive government financial assistance, and the Ruhr, where the companies initially pursued private measures. The unions strongly resisted plant closings, and by 1983-1987 the government had contributed $1.72 billion to restructuring (*Economist*, March 7, 1987).

Japan

Japan is the only country in this study, other than Canada, to increase its production between 1970 and 1990 (18 percent) at the same time that it also reduced employment by 44 percent.[6] The Japanese steel industry began to think about restructuring in 1978 in order to maintain its position in the world steel market. Several producers considered closing unnecessary plants and cutting back their capacity. The Nippon Steel Corporation (NSC), Japan's leader, made plans to shut down its Kamaishi plant, which employed 8,000 people and represented 80 percent of the local economy. By 1981, the prediction was for a decrease of 2 to 3 percent a year in output. The industry projected lower demand in Japan and overseas because of a recession in Europe and a generally sagging world economy. Sumitomo reported only six out of its ten blast furnaces were operating. However, technology was still improving and the newest Japanese steel plants could produce 1,800 tons of steel per man year at 90 percent capacity utilization, up from 1,000 tons per man year in 1977.

By 1984, only 39 of the nation's 65 blast furnaces were operating, and those only at 63 percent of their capacity. Because American producers had also suffered losses, the Japanese were forced to control their exports to the United States to avoid "dumping" charges. Overall, steel production had risen to 106 million tons in 1984, while using only 65 percent of its capacity.

Japanese steelmakers experienced a further drop in production in 1986, due to the continued strength of the yen. This was coupled with strong competition from South Korea and a worldwide decline in demand. In response to this, NSC announced further cutbacks and plans to suspend at least three of its twelve blast furnaces over the next five years beginning in April 1987. Japanese steel production overall fell to 98.5 million tons. In February 1987, Kawasaki announced plans to shut down its rolled-steel mill in Chiba. In the same year, plans were announced for bringing Nippon Kokan (NKK), the second largest steel company, back to a position of profit-making by the end of March 1989. It was hoped that by the end of fiscal year 1991, NKK would once again be a world competitor. Its plan presumed that Japan's annual crude steel production would total about 90 million metric tons by 1990. NSC expected to suffer losses of about $650 million in 1987, but in November the steelmaker began to report slight recoveries and profits as domestic demand rose and employment was reduced. Out of NSC's twelve blast furnaces, five were idled and one reblown, bringing the total number operating to eight in 1990. Of NSC's eight integrated steelworks with blast furnaces, four were expected to be shut down.

Restructuring in Japan has taken the form of diversification, joint ventures, and a reduction of capacity. However, there has been a great deal of coordination of investment and policy intervention by the Ministry of International Trade and Industry (MITI) (Yamawaki 1988). Steelmakers initially pursued entry into new businesses that had some relationship to their traditional product. They began to sell their by-product gases to chemical companies as "feedstock," allowing the chemical companies to reduce their reliance on petroleum. NKK went into engineering and construction in the shipbuilding, bridge-building and pipeline construction industries. Foreseeing an expansion into oil and gas treatment, NKK began to construct liquid natural gas storage tanks, drilling facilities, and offshore platforms. NKK also developed a division dealing with the engineering and construction of iron and steelmaking equipment and pollution control facilities for improved working conditions. In 1976, NKK helped build a $52 million plant in the Soviet Union to produce 500,000 tons of steel

Japanese firms, because of their success, became a model for steel firms in other countries and began to use their experience to assist competitors with their restructuring. In 1981, Nuova Italsider, Taranto Steel Corporation of Italy, called in NSC for assistance in restructuring (Masi 1986). It was noted that the Kimitsu facilities were averaging 10 percent higher yields than Taranto, while consuming 12 percent less energy. Also, Kimitsu made better use of its equipment and achieved 20 percent greater output from its workforce. Kawasaki collaborated with Italy and Brazil to build an integrated steelworks in Tubarao, Brazil.

Diversification, however, was much broader than technology transfer. Steel companies went into joint ventures with foreign and domestic electronics and computer companies. One competitor joined with a steelmaker to produce silicon wafers for semiconductor gate arrays and very large scale integrations for telecommunications circuits. In some firms, such as NSC, diversification was from steel to chemicals and then engineering and electronics, information, communication, social and cultural development (urban redevelopment) and biotechnology. In the spring of 1990, NSC opened Space World, a theme park on the site of a closed plant.

The results from diversification have been mixed. High-tech businesses are difficult to master. NSC opened and then closed a mail-order business and shut an international business communications center. Ventures by NSC in electronics, specialty materials, and biotechnology are growing slowly.

Japanese firms, at the beginning of a major slump in demand in 1982, also began to enter into joint ventures in the United States (Peterson 1990). They sought access to U.S. markets, particularly to the business of their transplanted auto companies. In April of 1982, NSC joined with Reed Tubular Productions Company to establish Reed Nippon Corporation, a specialized tool manufacturing and drill-pipe processing company. Also in 1982, NKK began negotiating with Ford Motor Company to purchase its Rouge Steel plant outside Detroit. And, in December, the Toyota Motor Corporation and NSC jointly developed a new sheet steel for car bodies to prevent rust and corrosion, called Excelite. The metal is a bonded double layer of iron and zinc alloy.

NKK, the world's second largest steelmaker, agreed in 1984 to acquire 50 percent of National Steel's subsidiary National Intergroup Incorporated. NKK was to pay $292 million to National and the subsidiary was to be run as a joint venture. In 1990, NKK owned 90 percent of the sixth-largest steel producer in the United States.

On July 16, 1984, Kaiser Steel Corporation reported it had agreed to sell its Fontana Works to a joint venture between a Southern California business, a Brazilian company, and a Japanese company. The venture was to be called California Steel Industries, and the technical advisor was Kawasaki Steel Corporation. In December of 1985, Kawasaki Steel announced that it might raise its stake in California Steel from one-quarter to one-third of the ownership. Also in 1985, LSI Logic Corporation agreed with Kawasaki Steel Corporation to build a $100 million manufacturing plant in Japan to be called Nihon Semiconductor, Inc.

NKK and National planned in 1986 to invest in ceramics, polymer products, new metals development, and computer technology, rather than simple steel production. In 1986, NSC announced an agreement with an American company to investigate a new area of expansion and diversification of the steel industry in the field of producing super minicomputers in Japan.

On March 23 of 1987, NSC and Inland Steel Corporation were reported to have finalized their agreement to build a $400 million plant near South Bend, Indiana for an 800,000 ton-a-year coating plant.

The Japanese found a willing partner in the United States because U.S. steelmakers wanted access to Japanese technology.

Sweden

Swedish steel restructuring was characterized by the development of a single nationalized company, the Swedish Steel Corporation (SSAB), and the major role played by the unions. The full participation of the unions in restructuring was greater than in any other country in this study and is discussed in chapter 3. Production was reduced by 19 percent (see table 1.1) and employment by 35 percent (see table 1.2). Swedish steel had been suffering since the 1960s from declining profits due to increased competition from imports and losses in its overseas markets. Although Sweden is not a member of the European Common Market, its economy is closely tied to activities in the Common Market, and the situation for steel was quite similar to that of the other European steel-producing countries in this study.

Swedish steel restructuring began in February 1976. The steel industry council, composed of the integrated steel manufacturers, established a government-sponsored Commission of Inquiry on commercial steel to examine the possibilities for restructuring the industry (SSAB Annual Report 1978). The Commission presented its report in March 1977, proposing to raise productivity through changes at the crude-steel and rolling-mill stages. The Commission suggested that the production of market-ready steel should be apportioned among the major rolling mills, which were owned by the three largest producers: Granges AB; Norrbottens Jarnverk AB, which was state-owned; and Stora Kopparbergs Bergslags AB. To supplement the Commission's work, the Ministry of Industry established the Steel-Town Group in May 1977, so that the county administrators could have input into the economic and employment effects of these recommendations on their communities.

After the Commission's report, the three major producers began talks about the formation of a single steel company. The Ministry of Industry and representatives of the central unions, particularly the LO (blue-collar) and the PTK (white-collar) union confederations, were involved in these discussions from the beginning. Under the Swedish Co-Determination Act, the unions were required to have a voice in all matters affecting the employees' welfare. An agreement to form SSAB was signed in December 1977. The government would own 50 percent and Granges and Stora 25 percent each. This agreement also included projected financial support from the government, which was crucial in the deal because of two reconstruction loans, totaling $687 thousand, and a capital projects loan of $235 thousand.[7] The Swedish Parliament agreed to support the restructuring in April 1978, but stipulated that employment in all the affected companies would be unchanged until March 31, 1983. The three companies merged in May 1978, retroactive to January 1, 1978, after considerable negotiation over the respective values of the facilities that the two private companies had contributed to the new company. This was important to the private firms because it would determine their percentage of ownership of the new company. The value of the carbon steel plants was exchanged for shares in SSAB. Each company contributed $156 million, all carbon steel plants, and equipment. Norrbottens Jarnverk AB, which was state-owned, contributed an additional $155 million in cash for the remaining 50 percent of the shares. Restructuring also covered the mines and railroad owned by Granges and the mines owned by Stora. The government loan was used to buy the railroad, which became part of Swedish Rail. These mines and railroads had been the source of losses for the private firms.

One estimate of the cost of the additional guarantee of no change in employment from March 1981 to March 1983 was $64 million (SSAB Memo). The first structural plan calculated that 3,500 jobs would be eliminated and perhaps 2,000 created. All personnel in the three companies initially received offers of employment on unchanged terms. However, if the government required SSAB to take steps which would involve the Swedish labor market policy, SSAB would be compensated.

SSAB's initial strategy for reorganizing was to make Domnarvet the strip and sheet manufacturing facility, Oxelösund the heavy gauge and industrial plate facility, and Lulea the heavy and medium gauge facility. The billets would come from Lulea and Oxelösund. The mining operations would be severely reduced, since domestic ore could not match imported iron ore prices, and most of the mines were closed. Overall, some operations would be shut down at each of the three sites to reduce excess capacity by 25 percent or 3.1 million tons and to adjust to the projected international and domestic markets. At the same time, new investments would be made at some of the facilities and there would be a changeover to the more efficient continuous casting. SSAB's plan was to move towards an integration of the three facilities into a single company.

A new strategy was adopted in August 1981, based on the continued poor international market for steel. After negotiations among the three owners, Stora Kopparberg's shares were purchased by the government, which now had a 75 percent stake, and Granges, which had a 25 percent stake. The government and Granges both agreed to increase their equity capital, close the mines, and allocate products among the three sites. The government had also funded SSAB by $872,611 billion (1982 $ US) in reconstruction loans, debenture loans, and equity capital. The new five-year plan called for the reduction of crude steel capacity by 25 percent in order to increase productivity and decrease costs in the remaining capacity. The blast furnace at Domnarvet was closed and dismantled.

SSAB's annual report at the end of 1982 listed a profit of $4 million (1982 $ US), after depreciation and interest. SSAB (Annual Report 1982) attributed these results to "cost reduction, mainly ascribable to the concentration of production to fewer units, the adoption of more efficient technology, and sheer hard work." It also projected a new five-year plan into 1987, in which it would seek to further reduce costs through continued restructuring and the introduction of new technology. New investments were allocated among the divisions.

By the mid-1980s, however, SSAB was having a new crisis. Management had relinquished control of distribution channels, entered into a number of company takeovers, and encountered difficulties in restructuring. The board and chief executive were replaced at the end of 1986, and a new plan for restructuring was drawn up. This new plan differed considerably from the early restructuring plans, and there were serious differences of opinion between the unions and management and among the unions themselves (Larsson 1987). The unions wanted to develop SSAB rather than close down more facilities. They didn't want to concentrate on sheet steel or to place SSAB on the stock market. Government support continued to subsidize operating expenses, with grants totaling $857 thousand in 1986 (SSAB Annual Report 1986).

At the end of 1986, the government agreed to purchase Granges' 25 percent holding, and the state then sold a third of the shares in SSAB to a consortium of pension funds. A plan proposed in 1987 called for the closing of the mines at Grangesberg and Dannemona, innovation in the steelmaking units of Lulea, Oxelösund, and Domnarvet (so that steel was completely ore-based and sheets could be manufactured for flat products), and closing of the electric steel mill in Domnarvet.

The European Economic Community

EEC steel policies are based on the 1951 Treaty of Paris, which led in 1953 to the establishment of the European Coal and Steel Community. Coal and steel were expected to lead the way to further economic integration.

The sharp change in demand and decline in steel prices provoked a call for community action early in 1975. In that year, producers were asked to give monthly notification to the Coal and Steel Commission of actual and likely employment. The history of steel restructuring in the EEC is a gradual move from voluntary action to mandated quotas, since the problem was both political and economic. The metal unions were an important source of support for the political parties and therefore unemployment was also a political issue. European parliamentary governments were reluctant to proceed with plant closings, which could cause a bitter struggle and social unrest. The Thatcher government's battles to close coal mines and steel mills were risks that other European governments chose not to take.

The objective was to restore the competitive position of the EEC companies. The Coal and Steel Commission first undertook short-term measures to bolster steel prices through voluntary approaches, such as reductions in supply and production and the issuance of minimum process and guidance prices. With a few minor changes, this voluntary system was extended or renewed in December 1975 and again in December 1979. Voluntary commitments to limit production were very difficult to achieve among the member countries because the steel industry represented the powerful interests of both the firms and the unions at home.

In 1978, the Coal and Steel Commission signed 15 voluntary agreements on export restraints with the main foreign suppliers of steel to the Community. This was part of the anticrisis plan where surplus capacity was not seen as a temporary phenomenon but rather as a structural problem, and steel producers were strongly encouraged to close down their old and inefficient plants. The reduction of productive capacity in the steel sector was to be accompanied by investment in new technology to raise productivity and competitiveness. Plans for reductions, however, did not prevent the member countries from assisting their own firms with subsidies allowing them to continue to produce at prices not sufficient to meet average costs. Fear of employment loss, as well as the need to preserve national self-sufficiency in steel, prompted the member countries to continue their help.

The Coal and Steel Commission believed its main task was to promote the restructuring of European steel. The leverage it used was control over subsidies for innovation, and it held out the promise of social funds for employees. Between December 1974 and 1981, 245,000 steelworkers lost their jobs in the EEC, with Britain, France, Belgium, and Luxembourg carrying the main burden of adjustment in the form of plant closures. In 1980, the European Coal and Steel Commission imposed mandatory quarterly production quotas and laid down guidelines on price increases by steel product. A code in state aids called for governments to end all subsidies, interest rebates, and capital and loan guarantees to the steel companies by the end of 1985 and provided the Coal and Steel Commission with the basis for closing the least viable plants. The system of monitoring the steel industry and setting production quotas is known as the Davignon Plan, named after Etienne Davignon, the European Community's commissioner for industrial policy. The move to mandatory quotas to force downsizing was based on the forecast that world economic growth rates would be low, world consumption of steel would decline, and reserves of steel capacity would continue to exist in Japan and the most efficient EEC producers. The Coal and Steel Commission would give aid or its approval only if the capacity increases resulting from proposed investment were offset by capacity reductions elsewhere.

Production quotas under the Davignon Plan were based on the maximum production estimates for 1980. See table 2.1 for these quotas. By January 1984, each member state was to inform the EEC of how it planned to restructure, that is, which plants would be shut down. Voluntary reductions made by the Common Market countries since 1980 were counted towards the required reductions in capacity. It can be inferred from table 2.1 that the greatest efforts at restructuring prior to the Davignon Plan had been achieved by Germany, France and Great Britain.

At the same time that the EEC was moving towards mandated quotas, member governments were still responding to internal pressure from powerful interest groups to increase government assistance. The Coal and Steel Commission, in order to reduce the impact of this continued assistance, mandated the end of all aid after 1985. In January 1984, the Commission agreed to a two-year extension of steel production quotas designed to share orders in Europe's depressed steel market. By 1985, however, pressures began to build on the Coal and Steel Commission to return the steel industry to free market conditions, and the Coal and Steel Commission agreed to a plan that would gradually make steel production dependent on market conditions. Further cuts in capacity though plant closures were resisted by the members, who argued that this might require closing of their only rolling mill.

The EEC countries, with the exception of Great Britain, have historically avoided reducing employment through layoffs and discharges. These countries first attempt to maintain employment either through transfers or retraining or to soften the effects of employment reductions through voluntary resignations, and then to encourage both early and normal retirements. Table 2.2 presents data on employment displacements in steel for the four EEC countries of this study from 1980 to 1988 by how the displacement took place. The data support one of the hypotheses that follows from the comparative industrial relations systems matrix that Great Britain used dismissals, while Belgium, Luxembourg, and West Germany preferred to reduce steel employment through retirement.

Table 2.1
Common Market Steel Industry Quotas by Country

Country	Maximum possible production in 1980 (percent in parentheses) Tons (000)	Closures made and capacity reductions volunteered by member states since 1980 Tons (000)	Contribution called for by commission Tons (000)	Contribution plus reductions since 1980 (percent in parentheses) Tons (000)
Federal Republic of Germany	53,117 (31.6)	4,810	1,200	6,010 (11.3)
Belgium	16,028 (9.5)	1,705	1,400	3,105 (19.4)
Denmark	941 (0.6)	66	n.a.	66 (7.0)
France	26,869 (15.9)	4,681	630	5,311 (19.7)
United Kingdom	22,840 (13.5)	4,000	500	4,500 (19.7)
Italy	36,294 (21.5)	2,374	3,460	5,834 (16.1)
Luxembourg	5,215 (3.1)	550	410	960 (18.4)
Netherlands	7,297 (4.3)	250	700	950 (13.0)
Total	168,601	18,436	8,300	26,736

SOURCE: European Economic Community, *Economic Community Bulletin*, 6-1983, p. 9.

Table 2.2
EEC Steelworker Reductions by Type, 1980-1988

Year	Dismissals	Voluntary resignations	Retirements	Early retirements	Other reasons	Total
Belgium						
1980	588					588
1981	376	492	1,154	1,104		3,126
1982	240	295	1,869	1,838	1,633	5,875
1983	919	223	1,067	989	1,126	4,324
1984	994	177	2,229	2,186	1,727	7,313
1985	250	175	2,753	2,708	1,291	7,177
1986	454	233	3,354	3,314	1,577	8,932
1987	1,653	183	693	657	1,057	4,243
1988	347	229	897	823	1,474	3,770
Total	5,821	2,007	14,016	13,619	9,885	45,348
Great Britain						
1980	40,039					40,039
1981	13,739	1,773	9,037	8,515		33,064
1982	7,816	1,133	5,166	4,940	3,047	22,102
1983	6,846	717	3,796	3,689	3,312	18,360
1984	1,687	822	1,006	880	2,156	6,551
1985	2,094	836	1,241	1,054	1,734	6,959
1986	2,029	850	1,647	1,372	1,540	7,438
1987	1,045	734	1,148	875	1,093	4,895

1988	333	779	1,029	725	1,287	4,153
Total	75,628	7,644	24,070	22,050	14,169	143,561

Luxembourg

1980	35	315	603	255		350
1981	40	312	1,150	782	1,865	1,210
1982	20	312	1,075	829	914	4,129
1983	31	342	713	522	1,094	3,191
1984	13	396	743	514	615	2,738
1985	18	140	726	528	337	2,030
1986	25	92	851	527	750	1,727
1987	27	113	834	578	413	2,268
1988	31	158				2,014
Total	240	2,180	6,695	4,535	5,988	19,657

West Germany

1980	4,123					4,123
1981	3,904	5,835	5,370	4,380		19,489
1982	2,479	3,033	6,721	5,832	10,795	28,860
1983	2,029	1,781	8,923	7,597	7,268	27,598
1984	942	1,582	10,243	9,588	12,091	34,446
1985	902	1,619	4,610	3,939	7,723	18,793
1986	1,398	2,049	8,527	7,811	9,746	29,531
1987	2,841	1,888	5,477	4,771	9,491	24,468
1988	984	4,054	1,844	3,333	9,861	17,866
Total	19,602	19,631	53,925	47,251	66,975	205,174

Table 2.2 (continued)

Total Four Countries

Year	Dismissals	Voluntary resignations	Retirements	Early retirements	Other reasons
1980	44,785	315	16,164	14,254	
1981	18,059	8,412	14,906	13,392	17,340
1982	10,555	4,773	14,861	13,104	12,620
1983	9,825	3,063	14,191	13,176	17,068
1984	3,636	2,977	9,347	8,215	11,363
1985	3,264	2,770	14,254	13,025	13,200
1986	3,906	3,224	8,169	6,830	12,391
1987	5,566	2,918	6,814	5,459	13,035
1988	1,695	3,010			
Total	101,291	31,462	98,706	87,455	97,017

SOURCES: European Economic Community, Eurostat, *Employment and Unemployment*, 1988, p. 177 and UECSC, Employment—*Iron and Steel*, 1987, p. 4.

Financial assistance was the carrot used by the EEC to force the downsizing. Based upon the Coal and Steel Treaty of 1951, assistance is provided "if the introduction of new technical processes or equipment should lead to an exceptionally large reduction in labor requirements in the coal and steel industry, making it particularly difficult in one or more areas to re-employ redundant workers." The Commission may pay for unemployment (tide-over) allowances, resettlement allowances and vocational retraining. The same aid is available if there are "fundamental changes." European Coal and Steel Community funds may be used to pay allowances in order to "enable them to continue paying such of their workers as may have to be temporarily paid as a result of the industry's change of activity." This aid, which comes from an annual tax on coal and steel firms, is nonrepayable and is conditional upon matching funds by each country. Financial aid was extended by the Treaty of Rome (1952), which provided for the establishment of a European Social Fund with the task "of rendering the employment of workers easier and of increasing their geographical and occupational mobility within the Community."

The quotas imposed in the 1980s were backed up by the social programs begun in 1984. Aid from the Social Fund and Readaptation Aid were made available for: voluntary early retirement, short-time working, tide-over allowances, training and retraining, severance pay, and other benefits. Table 2.3 presents the data on Social Fund commitments to the four EEC countries of this study for 1973-1985.

Comparisons among the four countries in their use of the Social Fund are difficult because of the differences in the size of their employment reductions. Germany had 31.61 percent of the total employment reduction between 1974-1984, and during this same period received 55.21 percent of the total Social Fund disbursement. For the same period, the figures for Great Britain are 52.69 percent and 40.00 percent, respectively. Great Britain appears to have used less of the total appropriations, although its job losses were greater than West Germany's. There is some discussion in the literature that the BSC and the British government failed to apply for all of the Social Fund's monies to which they were entitled (Iron and Steel Confederation).

Readaptation Aid to steelworkers was in the form of income maintenance during unemployment, supplements to early pensions, training allowances, mobility assistance, severance payments and short-time

46

Table 2.3
Social Fund Commitments for Steel in the Four EEC Countries, 1973-1985
(Millions of $ US)

Year	Belgium	Great Britain	Luxembourg	West Germany	Total
1973	8.50	67.78	.05	23.55	99.88
1974	8.22	78.30	.01	35.12	121.65
1975	9.35	128.46	.03	48.63	186.47
1976	8.87	120.22	.08	50.19	179.36
1977	13.29	305.05	.17	91.29	409.81
1978	15.83	159.32	.50	85.72	261.37
1979	22.98	283.23	1.44	76.25	383.90
1980	38.37	309.72	1.22	141.38	490.69
1981	25.17	270.27	.61	81.00	377.05
1982	22.81	428.28	.45	88.23	539.77
1983	26.05	455.14	.79	88.17	570.15
1984	63.39	616.81	.36	58.41	738.97
1985	93.27	494.13	.80	100.55	688.75
Total	356.10	3,716.71	6.51	968.49	5,047.81 [a]
Percentage	7	74	1	19	

SOURCE: Commission of the European Communities, Report from the Commission to the Council, *Eleventh Report on the Activity of the European Social Fund*, June 30, 1983, Eurostat for 1983-85 data.

NOTE: The ECU's have been converted to $ US. The ECU to $ US exchange rate used in this table and tables 2.4 and 2.5 for the years prior to 1979 was furnished by Eurostat.

a. Does not sum to 100 because of rounding.

working. Part of the EEC's contributions were financed by a special
program for steel begun in 1981. The data in table 2.4 indicate that
Great Britain and Germany, with the largest steel employment,
received the most Readaptation Aid. Great Britain used less of the
Social Fund and more of the Readaptation Aid than Germany. Great
Britain received 79 percent of the funds for 48 percent of the workers,
while Germany received only 14 percent of the total aid for a slightly
smaller proportion, 43 percent, of the total workers.

A study of Readaptation Aid concludes that "tide-over allowances"
or income maintenance during unemployment became an early retirement aid (Commission of the European Communities 1988). That is,
workers drew it until early retirement payments were received. As
income maintenance, it was useful only for younger workers who
sought new jobs. Social security systems also affected the type and use
of Readaptation Aid in each EEC country. In Great Britain and Belgium, Readaptation Aid was used as a substitute for social security
payments. In other countries, it served as a small subsidy to top off the
system. The study also concludes that Readaptation Aid made the
restructuring process more acceptable by reducing the costs to the government and the firms. This allowed firms to make concessions to the
unions and created a better climate for the unions to accept restructuring.

The EEC's contribution could make up as much as 50 percent of the
cost of general assistance and was concentrated in income supports
such as early retirement rather than job creation. In Luxembourg,
reemployment into a lower-paid job was subsidized for 18 months.
Income support paid a percentage of the difference between the old
wage and the new wage (95 percent for the first six months, 90 percent
for the next six months and 85 percent for the final six months). Early
pensions in Luxembourg covered up to three years and as high as 85
percent of the former wage for 12 months, 80 percent for 12 months
and 75 percent for 12 months. The EEC's contribution for the first year
would have been 50 percent of the difference between unemployment
benefits and 85 percent of the former wage, for the second year 50 percent of the difference between two times the unemployment benefits
and 80 percent of the former wage, and for the third year, 50 percent of
the difference between 0.8 times unemployment benefits and 75 percent of the former wage.

Table 2.4
EEC Readaptation Aid for Steel, 1954-1983
($ US)

	Country										
	Belgium		Great Britain		Luxembourg		West Germany		Total	
Year	Aid	Workers covered	Aid	Workers covered	Aid	Workers covered	Aid	Workers covered	Aid	Workers covered
1954-75a	4,665,292	10,790	567,544	1,139	13,532	220	4,665,292	42,118	9,991,660	54,267
1976	2,942,937	1,957	2,084,128	2,633	n.a.	n.a.	821,364	2,286	5,848,428	6,876
1977	841,616	526	2,110,472	2,792	n.a.	n.a.	273,495	521	3,225,583	3,839
1978	3,201,590	1,619	15,666,141	13,025	1,924,878	541	1,089,112	3,381	21,881,721	18,566
1979	2,534,860	812	31,158,378	14,366	1,531,658	894	6,042,282	7,691	41,267,178	23,763
1980	129,977	n.a.	63,181,325	20,102	3,744,801	450	3,249,445	3,656	70,305,549	24,208
1981	n.a.	n.a.	95,714,369	29,258	303,670	193	17,953,006	10,783	113,972,040	40,234
1982	n.a.	n.a.	58,388,115	12,102	n.a.	n.a.	9,301,049	8,264	67,689,163	20,366
1983	3,539,824	1,317	51,592,113	7,392	n.a.	n.a.	13,283,700	12,769	68,415,638	21,478
Total	17,856,096	17,021	320,462,585	102,809	7,519,539	2,298	56,678,745	91,469	402,516,960	213,597
Percentage	4	8	80	48	2	1	14	43		

SOURCE: Commission of the European Communities, mimeographed, Brussels.

a. ECU = 1.06981 $ US in 1964.

n.a. = Not available.

Funds for income maintenance, which relieved the pressure on the unemployment insurance funds of each of the countries, amounted to $669 billion for 317,555 workers in the four countries from 1954 to 1990. The largest percentage went to Great Britain, although Germany had the largest percentage of workers covered. Table 2.5 presents income maintenance expenditures.

The Coal and Steel Commission debated the production quota and capacity reduction issues for several months. Finally, in January 1988, it decided to exclude steelmakers with an annual output of less than 200,000 tons from the quota system and to extend the quota system for other steelmakers until June 1988, at which time the quota system would end entirely (*Wall Street Journal*, January 7, 1988). The use of quotas and employment reductions were never fully accepted by EEC members. Some countries, such as Germany, thought that they had made severe voluntary reductions in steel output while their neighbors, such as Italy, had ignored the quotas, expanded production, and still prospered. One of the principal incentives for restructuring was the offer of the Social Fund monies transferred from the EEC general treasury. When the EEC council refused to transfer any more of these funds, one of the major incentives for reductions in capacity was eliminated, and the quota system ended. After five years of production quotas, 1980-1985, the steel community had taken 23 percent of its hot-rolling capacity out of use, and after eight years, 1980-1988, it had eliminated 280,000 jobs.

Conclusions

How well did the characteristics of the adversarial and cooperative categories describe what actually happened in the eight countries on the issue of restructuring and the role of government? Figure 2.2 presents a comparative summary of restructuring and illustrates the conclusion that restructuring in the various countries did not always fit the expectations of the typology.

The Canadian steel industry combines characteristics of both the adversarial and the cooperative categories, since there are several large private firms and several small public firms. The private firms restruc-

Table 2.5
Income Maintenance for Steel in EEC Countries 1954-1990
($ US)

Year	Belgium Income	Belgium Workers covered	Great Britain Income	Great Britain Workers covered	Luxembourg Income	Luxembourg Workers covered	West Germany Income	West Germany Workers covered	Total Income	Total Workers covered
1954-75	2,945,292	10,790	6,547,709	12,059	13,532	202	4,665,292	42,118	14,171,825	65,169
1976	813,452	610	2,084,131	2,633	n.a.	n.a.	821,364	2,286	3,718,947	5,520
1977	4,370,402	2,986	2,110,411	2,792	n.a.	n.a.	273,495	521	6,754,308	6,299
1978	3,350,982	2,186	15,666,141	13,025	1,924,878	541	1,089,112	3,881	22,031,113	19,633
1979	772,858	472	31,158,378	14,366	1,531,658	894	6,041,561	7,691	39,504,455	23,423
1980	614,202	610	63,181,325	20,102	3,744,801	450	3,249,445	3,656	70,789,773	24,818
1981	2,652,500	2,354	95,714,369	29,258	304,670	193	17,953,006	10,783	116,624,545	42,588
1982	1,924,272	1,142	58,388,115	12,102	n.a.	n.a.	9,301,047	8,624	69,613,434	21,868
1983	2,662,573	1,756	51,592,113	7,392	n.a.	n.a.	13,283,700	12,769	67,538,386	21,917
1984	1,481,069	807	10,240,061	1,770	6,419,444	6,087	10,839,258	9,332	28,979,832	17,996
1985	8,242,376	4,285	17,071,209	4,477	4,275,461	n.a.	15,288,972	10,490	44,878,018	19,252
1986	269,206	332	10,390,105	2,891	n.a.	n.a.	27,993,101	9,133	38,652,412	12,356
1987	3,757,377	1,716	11,068,473	2,161	n.a.	n.a.	4,587,968	1,459	19,413,818	5,336
1988	974,724	125	8,701,279	1,123	3,900,068	1,100	50,692,671	13,162	64,268,742	15,510
1989	306,045	141	3,332,277	595	n.a.	n.a.	19,038,382	4,603	22,676,704	5,339
1990	1,085,197	297	7,167,510	1,606	11,184,132	3,217	19,897,761	5,411	39,334,600	10,531
Total	36,222,527	30,600	394,413,606	128,352	33,298,644	12,684	205,016,135	145,913	668,950,912	317,555
Percentage	5	9.6	59	40.4	5	4	31	46		

SOURCES: Commission of the European Communities, mimeographed and Annex to the *1990 Report on the Activities of the ECSC Readaptation Aid*, Brussels, December 1991.

tured without government support, while the public firms received support, particularly from the provincial governments. Canada did not undertake a great deal of restructuring. It added to capacity slowly and suffered less from the crisis than the other countries studied, particularly since it had a steady domestic market and the U.S. auto firms as customers.

Figure 2.2
Comparative Restructuring

| Categories and countries | Environmental issues | | Outcomes |
	Financial assistance	Initiative	Form of restructuring
Adversarial			
Canada	Private and provincial governments	Management	New technology
Great Britain	Government	Management	Plant closings
United States	Private	Management	Plant closings, mergers, diversification
Cooperative			
Belgium and Luxembourg	Government	Government	Plant closings, mergers
Germany	Private and state government	Government	Mergers, plant closings, diversification
Japan	Private	Management, government	Partial plant closings, shifting of products among plants, diversification
Sweden	Government	Management, government	Mergers

At first glance, the British steel industry appears to closely resemble the cooperative category. BSC, a publicly owned firm, received large-scale loans, most of which were forgiven. In practice, however, the company behaved very much as an adversarial enterprise in developing its own strategies, closing plants, eliminating jobs, and bargaining tough with the unions. In these activities, it received the support of both Conservative and Labor governments who had no choice when faced with the company's survival. Britain undertook deep restructuring and eliminated plants and jobs.

The U.S. steel industry fits the adversarial category well, since it restructured without government assistance. There were some exceptions in the form of import protection, trade adjustment assistance, and investment tax credits. The United States undertook deep restructuring with mergers, plant closings, job cuts, and diversification.

Belgium and Luxembourg fit the cooperative category well, since there was often tripartite decisionmaking. Belgian firms, particularly Cockerill-Sambre, received considerable government assistance, while Luxembourg steel restructured without aid for new capital but with aid for workforce reductions.

Germany fits both the adversarial and cooperative categories since the large companies restructured at first without government assistance, while the smaller firms in the Saar received considerable government aid in the form of loans, particularly from the state governments. The German firms vocally protested the receipt of government aid by their competitors in the other EEC countries; however, by the middle of the 1980s, the German government was supporting creation of two steel centers. Germany undertook restructuring by modernizing and diversification.

Japan resembles the adversarial category and to some extent the cooperative category. A small number of large firms compete within a cartel headed by Nippon Steel. Government aid is not in the form of loans, but through the encouragement of planning from MITI, which acts as a source of data-gathering and dissemination. Japan undertook restructuring by downsizing, diversification, and reductions in jobs.

Sweden fits the cooperative category, since the merger of three firms into one was undertaken after government loans were assumed and government aid continued.

NOTES

1. All financial statistics presented in the text or tables were converted to US dollars based on the period average of the exchange rate reported by the International Monetary Fund (1990). It should be noted that these dollar values will fluctuate with changes in currency market exchange rates and can distort comparisons because they do not take account of different price levels.

2. For a review of the U.S. competitive position, see National Research Council (1985) and Crandall (1981).

3. See Capron (1986) for a detailed discussion of the changes in the Belgium steel industry.

4. Leon-Ulric Houard, Personnel Director, S.A. Cockerill (May 1984).

5. See *Economist* (April 20, 1985 and July 13, 1985) and Graham (1983) for a discussion of the plan.

6. Japanese employment figures do not include large numbers of contract workers. If contract workers were included, employment levels would have been higher in 1970 and subsequent reductions much larger.

7. Orvar Nyquist, Executive Vice President of SSAB (May 1986).

3
Collective Bargaining
in Adversarial Countries

This chapter discusses how the bargaining process and the relationship among employers, unions, and government affected restructuring in adversarial countries. The United States section includes a case study of restructuring at the Fairfield, Alabama plant of United States Steel (USS). John P. Hoerr (1988) concluded that the Fairfield agreement set a pattern for the industry in labor relations and new concessions by other local unions around the United States. Expectations from the comparative systems matrix for the adversarial countries are that employers and unions would bargain over the impact of restructuring on the workforce, and that unions would not participate in corporate strategy decisions. Unions in these countries are expected to hinder adjustment and raise the costs of restructuring.

Canada

Collective bargaining in Canada is decentralized. Between 1974 and 1981, over 90 percent of the workers who bargained were in a single union bargaining structure, and 70 percent were in a single union/single employer structure (Gunderson and Meltz 1987). Collective bargaining has remained relatively stable over the past decade, and union membership has grown from 1974 to 1985, particularly in the public sector. This growth is related to favorable economic factors and public policy changes. The unions have been more militant than their U.S. counterparts, and labor disputes increased from 1965-1983 relative to 1946-65.

Roy J. Adams (1988) characterized industrial relations at Stelco as conservative and adversarial over the years. He maintained that the steps the company took to turn itself around in the mid-1980s were nothing "new" and well within the bounds of the traditional labor-management relationship practiced at the company. This traditional relationship at Stelco includes an accord agreed upon in the 1940s whereby Stelco made no attempt to undermine the union. If new plants are opened, there is a general understanding that management will voluntarily recognize the steelworkers as the bargaining agent. The union, on its part, makes no efforts to get involved in strategic decisions.

Bargaining became more centralized in the 1980s. The United Steelworkers of America (USW) locals formed a joint committee. However, Local 1005 at Stelco's Hilton Works still provided the leadership. It is considered one of the most militant locals in Canada. Traditionally, the Hilton Works, the company's largest site and an integrated mill, has set the wage and benefit pattern for the rest of the company, as well as for Dofasco, its closest competitor. Dofasco, a nonunion company, has consistently paid its workers the same rates as Stelco (Williams 1988).

A strike occurred in 1981 at the Hilton Works, located in Hamilton, Ontario. It involved approximately 12,800 workers and lasted for 125 days from July 31, 1981 to December 3, 1981 (Adams 1988). The dispute occurred in the context of joint and coordinated bargaining involving other Stelco plants and the United Steelworkers locals, which idled approximately 18,000 employees at 15 plants in 10 different locations. The Hilton Works local, as in previous negotiations, was part of a bargaining structure that included two-tier joint bargaining. The Stelco plants coordinated their bargaining with the locals at Algoma, the other major unionized firm in the industry. The pattern was that the Hilton Works Local 1005 would negotiate on economic issues for all of the 16 Stelco plants that were organized. This pattern would not be broken until 1988. Adams (1988) argues that at Stelco, management was able to react to market shifts quickly without union opposition, since it was operating within the terms of an adversarial collective agreement where unions do not participate in corporate strategy. He also maintains that the conditions at Stelco did not lend themselves to union avoidance, since union acceptance is assisted by the Canadian industrial relations environment.

Following the strike, Stelco's market share declined, employment costs rose, and Stelco's customers sought steel first domestically and then from the U.S. or Europe. Hilton has been important to Stelco and strikes at that plant, such as the one in 1981, were viewed by management as causes for losing customers. This strike coincided with a downturn in the Canadian economy, and the demand for steel declined. Firms that bought steel in the U.S. paid more than they had for Stelco's product. On the other hand, foreign competitors gained from the strike, and firms that purchased steel in Europe reported prices no higher than they were paying for Stelco steel, even after duty and transportation were included.

By 1984, the company had turned itself around, closing three finishing plants and a coal mine. They laid off 8,000 employees by 1986. In 1984, Stelco sought an early agreement to maintain uninterrupted production. This agreement was followed by layoffs and raised doubts in the membership's minds of the value of early settlements (Williams 1988).

Negotiations in steel take place at the local level. In 1984, when Stelco sought to reduce its workforce, close its Canada Works, and consolidate several process, it negotiated an agreement with the locals for the transfer of surplus workers to the finishing works. This agreement became the model for other plant closings in the company. The principal sections of the agreement included credit for full seniority when employees transferred; those employed prior to January 18, 1984 had rights to bid on jobs elsewhere, and if they were not employed as a result of bidding, they would be offered a job held by an employee hired after January 15, 1984. Finally, a joint implementation committee was created, made up of three local union officials and three managers.[1]

Stelco's reorganization in January 1988 into three companies was viewed by the union as an attempt to break the pattern coming from Hilton.

Great Britain

During the 1970s and 1980s, there was a definite trend toward decentralized bargaining. This was somewhat modified by the incomes policies, installed by the government during 1974-1979, which operated at the industry level. As political power has alternated between the Labor and Conservative parties from the early 1970s to the present, labor legislation has either been passed or revised to be consistent with the views of the political party in office (Bain 1987b).

The changes in union growth that started in Great Britain in the 1960s continued in this past decade. Trade union membership rose by over 3.2 million during the 1970s, and in 1979, reached a peak of 55 percent of the labor force. The decline in the traditional union sectors of shipbuilding, coal, and textile was more than offset by increases in the public sector. However, in the 1980s, this growth could not offset the loss of members in steel and coal (Price and Bain 1983).

Negotiations in steel were peaceful over the years. Most of the collective bargaining took place locally without industrywide negotiations. An arbitration procedure, established in 1969, referred local disputes to "neutral committees" consisting of two employer and two union representatives from another works. Steelworkers were represented by 18 unions. The Iron and Steel Trade Confederation, with a strength of 90,000 in 1980, represented about 50 percent of the workers. It can be considered a conservative union (Eason 1990). Other unions in steel included the National Union of Blast Furnacemen, which joined the Iron and Steel Trade Confederation in 1985, the Transport and General Workers Union, and the General and Municipal Workers Union.

When the British Steel Corporation (BSC) was formed in 1967, it found itself bargaining with 23 different unions at two levels of negotiations: national and local. These negotiations were formal, and the union branches were involved. Directors and union leaders might negotiate some broad agreements at the national level, but it was the local officers on each side who implemented, modified, or ignored them (Bamber 1984). Most aspects of blue-collar workers' jobs were regulated at the local level, including tonnage bonuses, manning agreements, and productivity agreements. For white-collar workers, general pay increases were negotiated at the national level by the unions, while the detailed salary structures were determined locally.

BSC management wanted to centralize negotiations with the unions, and the Trades Union Congress formed a Steel Committee composed of one representative from each of the six largest unions. The formation of the Steel Committee was crucial to restructuring, because it provided BSC with an institutional framework through which the problem of job loss could be negotiated (Bryer, Brignall, and Maunders

1982). Bamber argues that the unions had acquired control over the lines of promotion by exercising job control through seniority. The unions had a tradition of cooperating with the employers to exert power over the workplace, and Bamber says that this cooperation, combined with the unions' control over jobs, helped BSC to rationalize the industry without generally having to confront concerted union opposition (Bamber 1984).

Bryer, Brignall, and Maunders concluded that from BSC's creation, large-scale job losses were envisioned. One of the first agreements reached with the Steel Committee was on layoff procedures. They maintain that instead of questioning the rationale for the layoffs, the Steel Committee merely asked the government and BSC for help in managing them. The Trades Union Congress asked for earlier and further consultation over closures, help in dealing with local resistance from BSC senior managers when they visited the sites, and assistance in getting the Regional Industrial Directors through the Minister of Industry to survey the effects of plant decisions and set up joint regional committees. Bryer, Brignall, and Maunders said that the Steel Committee placed itself in a situation where it was shouldering all of the collective bargaining responsibility for the closures, including participation in BSC's job creation efforts.

A joint agreement in January 1976, allowed additional layoffs by shifting negotiations on manning levels to the plants. This is the same approach taken a little later by U.S. Steel at its Fairfield Plant. It provided BSC with the ability to negotiate early closings at the local level based on its ten-year development strategy (1973). Tradeoffs between jobs and retirement payments were easier to achieve at the local level.

The history of restructuring goes back to the Ten-Year Program of 1973. Under this plan, the industry was to be restructured by concentrating on the five large coastal "brownfield" sites of Ravenscrage, Teeside, Scunthorpe, Llanwern and Port Talbert. Redcar would be expanded, and many of the smaller sites would be reduced. There was also reaffirmation that the Beswick plants were high-cost and overmanned relative to international standards. The investment strategy in the 1973 plan for new technology and facilities was to be coupled with closings at inefficient facilities. However, by mid-1977, no closures had occurred because the Steel Committee and the Iron and Steel Trade

Confederation at the national level refused to accept closure where employment alternatives were not provided (Upham 1980). The results of BSC management's ability to shift negotiations to the local level were demonstrated when the local unions at the Clyde Iron Works concluded a plant agreement in 1977. This agreement gave them enhanced layoff payments for surrendering their jobs and broke the national united strategy of the unions. After the Clyde settlement, each site negotiated its own solutions. Within weeks, the Steel Committee, in order to regain some power, had negotiated a slightly better settlement for Hartlepool which closed that plant.

Most of the local unions traded retirement payments for jobs, since there appeared to be no prospect of keeping the mills open. What was negotiated was the structure of payments to favor the age structure of the workforce at the site (Grieves 1985). In March and April 1978, the East Moors site and the EbbwVale Steel Works were closed. In June 1978, Shelton was closed, even though there had been no national negotiations over its closing. Later that year, Bilston was temporarily kept open when the Iron and Steel Trade Confederation threatened a national strike if the plant was closed without an agreement with the union.

Plants didn't close without conflict, however, and local agreement was not always forthcoming. Some locals fought closing and resisted their national unions' attempts to negotiate peaceful closings. In February 1979, BSC announced that it wanted to close the Corby site, which had 5,500 employees (Maunders 1987). The plant was well organized with militant local unions, and local union officials did not invite the Steel Committee into town for a period of eight months. The local strategy was to establish a trade union policy group to look at ways of ensuring Corby's survival as an integrated works, and the policy group engaged academics from the University of Warwick and Cambridge. In September, the company and the local parties met, but BSC issued notice that they would close the plant in January 1980, and there was a community strike. In November, the unions presented a series of questions to management, and the unions withdrew from all consultation meetings including the works councils. Nevertheless, Corby was gradually closed during 1980 and the buildings torn down.

The collective bargaining relationship between the BSC and the Iron and Steel Trade Confederation could have been considered cooperative until 1979. However, the company's insistence that it had no more money to buy out plant closings with lump sum payments and still provide wage increases in plants that remained appeared to push the unions towards conflict. In the summer of 1979, the BSC proposed a consolidated pay settlement which amounted to about 2 percent, dating from Phase II of the Labor government incomes policy and also up to 10 percent in quarterly payments from local bonus plans. The union considered this merely the honoring of a commitment made the previous year. The bonus schemes appeared to the unions to put a ceiling on reward for improved performance and offered no guarantees. The local lump sum bonus plans put into place after the three-month 1980 strike were a bonus calculated at the end of each quarter based on the entire plant rather than the traditional shift-by-shift bonus. Management wanted to move to plant-level bargaining and more subcontracting among its plants. There was also conflict between the Steel Committee and the individual unions. The Committee, after nationalization, had emerged as the leading negotiator with BSC on nonpay matters such as pensions, holidays and job security; however, the individual unions did not want to surrender their bargaining rights to the Steel Committee with respect to pay, which included a system based on cost-of-living and production quotas.

Management and the unions appeared to be on a collision course, for while the unions had been gearing themselves for direct action, the BSC and its steel users had made their own preparations. The BSC sales force manned telephones on a 24-hour basis to ensure last minute steel supplies, and the BSC announced that "they were prepared to help customers by securing steel from other sources and arranged to import supplies from Europe if necessary" (*Financial Times*, December 21, 1979). By Christmas Eve 1979, most steel stockers had the equivalent of between 16 and 17 weeks' supply of steel in their warehouses.

The national steel strike of 1980, led by the Iron and Steel Trade Confederation, was the largest strike to occur in Great Britain since the Second World War, and the first national strike in the industry since 1926 (Docherty 1983; Hartley, Kelly, and Nicholson 1983). The strike was called by a union famous for its moderation after enormous pressure from the BSC-sponsored Thatcher government, which sought to accelerate the pace of closures and privatize steel. It lasted for 13 weeks and involved about 150,000 workers. The major issues were wages and jobs. The BSC offered steelworkers a 2 percent pay raise and local lump-sum bonuses tied to increases in productivity, rather than a national settlement. The company also wanted to trade these wage increases for job reductions and more closings. The Iron and Steel Trade Confederation felt they were being asked to meet the BSC losses through large- scale dismissals and moderate wage gains to support an investment strategy to which they had not been a party, and the union criticized the company for not involving it in strategic planning.

The strike ended on April 1, 1980, when the Iron and Steel Trade Confederation voted by a narrow majority to accept the recommendation of the Lever Commission of a 15.5 percent wage increase, 11 percent across the board and 4.5 percent from local productivity agreements. Local agreements, such as the one at Llanwern, provided for quarterly lump-sum bonuses and payments to those who would lose their jobs as a result of the "slimline" plan. These local bonus plans were negotiated across all the unions in the plant.[2]

Worker Directors

BSC experimented with an additional form of worker participation—worker directors. This form of participation was not legislated, as the works councils discussed in the next chapter, nor were their duties outlined. Still the evidence indicates they had moderate success. Worker directors were introduced experimentally at both the local level and on the main board in the BSC at its start-up.[3] Both management and labor supported the idea. The BSC chairman, Charles Villers, and the general secretary of the union of the Post Office Workers, who was a member of the BSC Board and advisor on the development of personnel, industrial relations, and social policy, were in favor of increasing worker participation in the running of the company. At the same time, the steel unions were pressing for worker input into strategic planning at each level of the company (Brannen 1983). The unions looked upon the nationalization of the steel industry as an opportunity to introduce the concept of sharing the power of managing with worker representatives. Worker directors were introduced on an experimental basis, and three worker directors were appointed to each of the four group boards. The Steel Committee received nominations from individual unions and created a short list of candidates to present to the BSC chairman, who appointed them. Attempts were made to ensure equitable representation by trade, occupation, and region. One criterion was that the individuals selected should have the necessary intellectual capacity to be acceptable members of the board. Extensive trade union and public service experience were taken not only as a proxy for this, but also as indicating familiarity with and ability to perform on committees and in the bureaucratic contexts. The worker directors tended to be older employees. Their average age was 55, and white-collar workers were overrepresented relative to their proportion of the workforce. The worker directors were appointed for a period of three years and paid at the same rate as nonexecutive directors. The worker directors continued with their normal employment when not engaged in board duties. Union positions had to be resigned, and the worker directors were not allowed to take part in parliamentary political parties or to disclose any confidential information.

Initially, the other directors of the British Steel Corporation were hostile to the concept of worker directors and saw their appointment as redundant and illegitimate. They had largely been opposed to the nationalization of the industry and saw the worker directors as another move towards employee ownership. However, when they were interviewed one year after the scheme had begun, a majority of directors favored the idea of worker directors. The majority of middle managers, employees, and union officials were also in favor of worker participation (Brannen 1983). But different groups attached different meanings to the concept of participation. These philosophical difficulties were reflected in attitudes towards worker directors. The major criticisms of the plan were that some viewed it as political, others as cosmetic, and there was a lack of accountability of the worker directors to either the shop floor or to the trade unions.

The 12 worker directors were reported to be very committed to their new role and displayed a great deal of enthusiasm. The boardroom was the main area of activity in the initial stages, and the worker directors were entering a symbolic world that had belonged to the full-time directors. They had to learn the language of the boardroom, its customs, its patterns of work organization, and its rules, as well as the customs for drinking and dressing. The interests of directors could be viewed as separating them from the interests of the workers. The social dynamic of the boardroom is to be a good board member; that is, to be a good director rather than a good worker. There were also pressures on the original board members to accommodate the new group and fit the new members into the regular board structure. Not to do so was to invite external threat to the board from the government and the unions, who had been responsible for nationalization, and internal instability within the board itself. The worker directors saw themselves as links between the senior management and the workforce, as well as the unions. They felt that the aim of the scheme was moving towards industrial harmony, and they laid stress on communication, mutual exchange of ideas, and the creation of a meeting point between management and the workforce.

The worker directors were sent to a five-week training course tailored to their specific needs, which was jointly organized by the Steel Industry Management College and the Steel Committee. Training was a version of a middle management course and spread out over two segments of two weeks and one final week. The worker directors were exposed to the management philosophy of the British Steel Corporation and its management techniques. During the breaks between training, the worker directors worked at their regular jobs. The objectives of the course were to provide: an appreciation of the national economic framework within which the steel industry operated; increased awareness of the issues facing the British steel industry, particularly the nationalized sector, and the organization and policies that the BSC was adopting; a discussion of some major aspects of trade union and Trades Union Congress policies; an introduction to modern thinking about management and relevant management techniques; an opportunity to formulate views about the role of the part-time director on group boards; and the opportunity to develop socially and personally in a learning environment (Banks and Jones 1977).

The training program enabled the worker directors to develop their own views as to what their roles as worker directors were. An initial job description was formulated for the worker directors. All full-time directors had functional responsibilities, and part-time directors were recruited for some special knowledge and influence. The worker directors were seen as experts on the shop-floor practice. This role limited their scope of action because issues related to labor relations formed a very small part of the board proceedings, and when they did, the focus was on the control of labor costs. There were several constraints on the worker directors, and they often found that they did not have the information the other directors had. To maximize the impact of their presence, the worker directors got involved in committees and working parties in order to successfully integrate themselves into the management structure. The director's role was strengthened at the expense of his worker role. Despite the condition of appointment that they drop involvement in union activities, the worker directors attempted to reestablish relations with their own unions and other unions. Their role as directors gave them a formal status and a degree of authority in relation to the management system; however, they had no formal status in relation to the trade union system.

The initial plan had several weaknesses, particularly the lack of a clear relationship between the worker directors and the trade unions. The experimental scheme was to be reviewed after the first three years in office, but because of the reorganization of the Corporation, it was decided to extend the experimental period to April 1972. The Corporation also decided in July 1968 that an independent academic study of the scheme was appropriate, and research was conducted by a team. Based on the report of the team, meetings were held between the Steel Committee and the BSC, with the result that a new job description was formulated. In 1973, it was agreed that the worker director idea should become a permanent feature of the BSC structure instead of an experiment. Several changes were made, including the greater involvement of the unions in the selection process for worker directors. The divisional directors of BSC also agreed that worker directors should not be barred from holding "non-negotiating" union posts. Discussions were opened with the unions, and it was decided that each union could select its own candidates to be considered by the Steel Committee, who then submitted a short list to a joint union-management committee. The joint committee then submitted the list of selected candidates to the chairman of BSC for final decision and approval. It was understood that where the joint committee was unanimous, the chairman accepted their view. Where there was disagreement, the chairman would make the final selection. This system operated for the first time in 1974 and ensured a better link between the worker directors and the trade union movement, as well as a higher degree of support for the worker directors.

In 1974, a BSC working party, which included worker directors, proposed to increase the number of worker directors at the divisional level and recommended appointing worker directors to the main board. The chairman proposed in 1975 that three worker directors be appointed to the main board: however, this suggestion was rejected by the government through the Secretary of State.

A second level of employee participation was encouraged by the Employment Act of 1982, which required companies employing more than 250 employees to include in the annual director's report information on action taken to introduce, maintain, or develop employee involvement. The BSC reported regular meetings with the Steel Committee. This committee reported that meetings had occurred at the national, "business" and local levels, but that it felt that these meetings had "very limited value." The Steel Committee argued that management didn't bring the unions into the formative stage but presented policy as an accomplished fact that had to be pursued in order to survive.

Collective bargaining, as related to restructuring, was characterized by a lack of cohesion among the unions in the BSC. Although the Iron and Steel Trade Confederation (ISTC) was dominant, the other 13 craft unions negotiated separately. It was not until 1982 that the 14 unions met, and not until 1983, after the strike, that they agreed on a joint wage strategy. The ISTC represented about half of the BSC employees, but this percentage shifted over time as plants closed, production declined, and workers were laid off. At the same time the Iron and Steel Trade Confederation attracted nonsteel workers whose numbers were increasing. This raises the question of whether the ISTC resisted layoffs as vigorously as it might have had it been faced with large losses in its total membership. Vaizey (1974) argued that the ISTC was traditionally under the control of a right wing group and identified with the objectives of management.

The Trades Union Congress attempted to overcome the problem of a lack of cohesion when it set up the Steel Committee, which coordinated the six largest unions. The BSC negotiated with the Steel Committee on employment but not over wages. During the course of plant closings there was even resistance by local union leadership to an appearance by the Steel Committee. The feeling was that if the Steel Committee was brought in, the priorities of the local plant workers would be compromised. The Steel Committee was caught by the strike without its own plan for restructuring. BSC management took the position that its poor competitive position, relative to steel producers in other countries, was primarily due to overmanning and high labor costs. The BSC sought to decentralize bargaining, while the Iron and Steel Trade Confederation advocated negotiations at the corporate level. In the 1970s, management committed itself to giving advance notice of plant closures. This was supposed to be a two-year notice, but was later shortened to one. After 1977, bargaining with regard to restructuring was decentralized. Management of those plants that were closing negotiated with the unions concerning the conditions of closures, including special compensation for the workers concerned without looking at the entire company picture. The ISTC came under pressure not to call a national strike over closings from those plants that were not faced with the problem.

Negotiating over payments to workers due to plant closings allowed the BSC to close plants sooner than the publicly announced dates. The payments were usually less than the full wages that BSC would have had to pay if the plants had stayed open to the last date. Finally, the workers at the threatened plants were more effective in resisting closings than the central structure of the trade unions. The local action committees were independent of the national leadership of the trade unions, and their main tactic was to hold a long series of meetings with the BSC in order to press the economic case for the retention of the threatened works in some form or other. The Youngstown Ecumenical Committee in the United States came closest to these action committees (Fuechtmann 1989).

United States

Collective bargaining in the United States during the 1970s may be characterized as following the principles and patterns of the New Deal Model developed in the post-World War Two years, and this was also true for steel (Kochan and Katz 1988). Since the organization of the integrated producers in the 1930s, collective bargaining has operated under the umbrella of the U.S. Steel Corporation and the United Steelworkers of America. The USW and the eight largest steel firms that formed the Coordinating Committee Steel Companies sought to maintain the status quo and prevent excessive competition in labor costs by industrywide bargaining.

Following a lengthy strike in 1959, when U.S. firms lost customers to foreign competitors, wage and benefit increases were uniform for bargaining rounds (Kalwa 1985). Steel firms were willing to pay more in labor costs rather than give up business and suffer from the frantic hedge buying that accompanied uncertain negotiations. On the union side, there is some futility to the use of a strike, since steel is not differentiated by company label (Fischer 1986). The steel crisis and the spector of rising imports in the 1970s drove "Big Steel" and the USW toward a limited form of cooperation. In 1973, the two sides signed the Experimental Negotiation Agreement, which granted an annual wage increase of 3 percent plus a cost-of-living adjustment (COLA) tied to the consumer price index, plus a bonus at the first signing. In exchange, workers pledged not to strike and to lend support to lobbying efforts against imports. The Experimental Negotiation Agreement was clearly an attempt to avoid crisis bargaining in an already sagging industry. However, negotiated increases were not coupled with capital improvements, and increases in productivity did not keep pace with increases in labor costs. As a result, real wages rose well in excess of productivity improvement. Between 1973 and 1979, wages in the mills rose 119 percent, compared with a 63 percent rise in the consumer price index (Kassalow 1984). At the same time, the rate of productivity improvement slowed; it had grown at only 2 percent per annum since 1962. By 1982, total hourly compensation in iron and steel was $23.78, or approximately double the average for all manufacturing. From 1976 to 1983, total compensation for production workers in steel increased by 94.5 percent, while for the same period for all manufacturing employees, the increase was 81.1 percent.

As the competitive position of the steel industry began to suffer in the 1970s, industrial relations altered. Firms were forced to look for ways to cut costs; they began to accept the idea that to survive they would have to bargain an agreement specific to their own company. In the late 1970s, attention turned toward serious reductions in labor costs, focusing on wage and benefit rates at the national level and on work rule issues at the local level. Work rules were seen as restrictive to competition because of their requirements for more manpower and jurisdictional restrictions over what tasks could be performed. There was a move to negotiate changes in manning levels, in jurisdictional rules, and in the combination of jobs. This was coupled with attempts to reduce wage and benefit levels and introduce more subcontracting arrangements into the workplace. Companies used the labor cost issue as the key to keeping a struggling facility open and as a bargaining chip in situations in which there was a choice of where to place new technology.

The 1980 agreement was considered an example of USW restraint. The total cost of the settlement was estimated at approximately 35 percent over three years. The union gained prenotification of plant closings, and the Experimental Negotiation Agreement was "decoupled" from the contract, with a decision on its renewal deferred (Kalwa 1985). The contract was reopened in July 1982, and August 1, the date of the next wage and cost-of-living increases, was set as a tentative deadline concerning "discussions" of the current contract. USW proposed diversion of scheduled raises to Supplementary Unemployment Benefits or lifetime security payments, investment in steel facilities, and employee stock ownership. However, the companies appeared to be dragging their feet by continuing to detail their financial situation without offering any specific proposals. In late July, the Coordinating Committee proposed a concession package, amounting to $6 billion worth of savings to be derived from cuts in COLA. The companies were adamant about the need for concessions, and negotiations were set against a background of company-initiated job combinations and eliminations and threats of plant closings throughout the industry. This led to hostility from the locals and rejection of proposed company concessions by the union at the end (Hoerr 1988). However, it appeared that management sought to achieve large concessions in a single bargaining round under U.S. Steel's aggressive leadership, and some of the other firms questioned this approach. The parties failed to reach agreement, but, returned to the table. The steel companies reaffirmed their united stand on labor policy, and continued layoffs resulted in a more conciliatory attitude from the USW. In September 1982, the USW convention recognized the need to balance wage gains with employment security, and they voted to resume negotiations. A key problem was COLA, which had accounted for 70 percent of wage gains since 1972. The issue was how to moderate COLA increases while retaining protection against inflation. In November 1982, the parties reached a tentative agreement, which would have reduced labor costs by 11 percent in the first year through a $1.50 per hour wage cut, elimination of two COLAs, and other concessions. The proposal was defeated in the union's Basic Steel Industry Committee, in spite of USW President McBride's support, by a 241-131 vote (Kalwa 1985). Two factors in its defeat were that many local presidents viewed concessions as futile in preventing layoffs and shutdowns, and the conference did not have adequate time for detailed deliberation concerning the proposals.

Negotiations began again in February 1983, after Roger Smith, chairman of General Motors, telephoned McBride and warned that steel contracts for the 1984 model year were to be awarded by March of 1983. The March 1 deadline was met after the USW agreed to concessions that amounted to 7 percent in labor cost savings in the first year. Costs were expected to rise by 11 percent over 41 months. Still, the immediate wage cut was reduced to $1.25 from the $1.50 sought in the ill-fated November 1982 negotiations, but it was a first in steelworker history (BNA 1983). The USW held firm on COLA, and only six periodic COLA adjustments were not made. The companies promised to avoid contracting out, and the union agreed to accept negotiated combination and elimination of jobs at the plant level. The companies also agreed to reinvest the labor cost savings in existing facilities, but were free to close down operations and the Experimental Negotiation Agreement was not renewed (Ahlburg et al. 1987). The USS purchase of Marathon Oil was the catalyst for the inclusion in this agreement that required the companies to invest all savings from the wage concessions in the modernization of steel (Block and McLennan 1985; *Business Week*, July 21, 1986).

As the union locals either resisted or adapted to management proposals, the structure of bargaining in basic steel began to disintegrate. Wheeling-Pittsburgh withdrew from the employers' Coordinating Committee, followed by Allegheny Ludlum and National Steel. In 1985, coordinated bargaining ended. The 1986 negotiations on a company-by-company basis were of two types. In one, companies felt that the only way to improve productivity was to seek a more cooperative arrangement with the union (Gerhart 1989; Sherer 1990). The second approach was taken by USS, which engaged in tough negotiations over reductions in labor costs. Settlements for the first group were arrived at peacefully. At LTV, Bethlehem, and Inland, the workers' take-home pay was reduced but concessions were offered in return. At National Steel, employment security and smaller wage reductions were agreed to, and the union guaranteed assistance and cooperation in reducing the workforce by a significant margin in future years. At USS, there was a six-month strike, which resulted in pay and benefit reductions of about 10 percent. USS succeeded in reducing their costs below those of Bethlehem, their largest competitor. At the same time that the companies began to negotiate separate agreements, plants and locals began to negotiate their own arrangements. Some of these plant differences appeared in national contracts, while others were confined to a single site. Negotiations at the USS Fairfield Works, just outside of Birmingham, Alabama, set a precedent for other local negotiations (Hoerr 1988).

The end of coordinated bargaining encouraged the decentralization of negotiations to the plant level. This created a problem for the USW leadership, which now had to reconcile its members' goals of preserving their jobs at each plant against the leadership's need for a coordinated strategy.

The Fairfield Works

Plant-level negotiations at the Fairfield Works in Alabama are an example of the relationship between restructuring and local negotiations in an adversarial setting and the tradeoff between site preservation and union concessions.[4] The five-year period covered by this case study is characterized by continuous requests by the company for reductions in manning, coupled with the threat of permanent closure. The union was caught between wanting to hold on to what they had previously achieved and not knowing whether each management request was to be the last concession, or whether, even with concessions, Fairfield would still close. The Fairfield Works is also an excellent example of how USS undertook restructuring one department at a time at a brownfield site. Figures 3.1 and 3.2 illustrate the production process and facilities prior to and after restructuring.

The Fairfield Works had been affected by the competitive pressures that began in the 1970s when the southern market for steel was hit hard

72

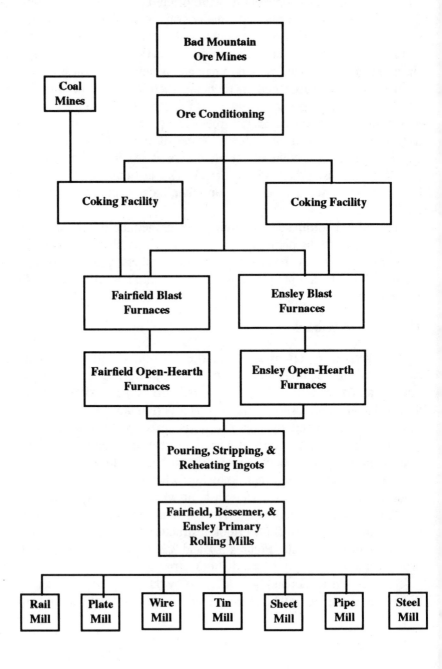

Figure 3.1
Fairfield and Ensley, 1970

Bad Mountain Ore Mines

Coal Mines

Ore Conditioning

Coking Facility

Coking Facility

Fairfield Blast Furnaces

Ensley Blast Furnaces

Fairfield Open-Hearth Furnaces

Ensley Open-Hearth Furnaces

Pouring, Stripping, & Reheating Ingots

Fairfield, Bessemer, & Ensley Primary Rolling Mills

Rail Mill

Plate Mill

Wire Mill

Tin Mill

Sheet Mill

Pipe Mill

Steel Mill

Figure 3.2
Fairfield, 1990

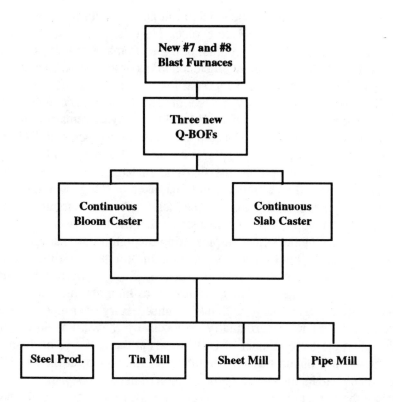

by foreign competition. USS announced the elimination of its Southern Division, which had been headquartered in Fairfield, and its absorption into the Eastern Division. Rumors began to surface that Fairfield would close.

In December 1978, the new 5,500-ton-per-day, number 8 blast furnace began operation, replacing older blast furnaces and ending a seven-year modernization program designed to make "hot-end" operations at Fairfield Works more efficient and in compliance with environmental standards. More than $500 million was spent between 1975 and 1978 on three new Q-BOFs, a huge, modern blast furnace, and a new battery of coke ovens. However, Fairfield employees remained unsure of what USS had planned. The company was in the process of deciding which of its product lines and plants would be closed as part of a rationalization plan. Stevenson, the Fairfield manager, in a letter to the employees, stated that "action had to be taken or things would not go on," hinting at a total shutdown of the facility. Stevenson reinforced his statements to employees by emphasizing that the letter was not meant to be a "scare tactic" aimed at pressuring the union into management-desired changes, but instead was meant to inform the employees of the severe crisis facing the Fairfield Works if changes were not made. Stevenson listed the problems at Fairfield as high absentee rates, frequent tardiness, and large amounts of unnecessary overtime. Maintenance workers were particularly criticized by Stevenson. Stevenson also cited the large number of USW locals at the mill—12 of them in 1979—as a problem that required change. Each plant at the site had originally had its own local. In the opinion of the company, more locals meant the consent of more local presidents over local issues and made the flexibility of work assignments difficult to attain. Figure 3.3 indicates the reduction in locals as a result of restructuring.

The union blamed plant problems on outdated equipment, excessive supervision and inexperienced managers. The company blamed the sites' problems on employee absenteeism and tardiness, excessive overtime and overmanning, and the large number of locals.

Table 3.1 presents the employment changes at Fairfield from 1955 through 1984 as the company restructured. It indicates a continuous reduction in jobs. Employees were laid off and sometimes recalled as the company modernized different stages of the production process. The largest reductions took place between 1955 and 1970, when capac-

Figure 3.3
Reduction in Locals at Fairfield, 1975-1984

Locals in 1975	Locals eliminated 1976-1980	Locals eliminated 1981-1984	Locals in 1984
1013 Steelmaking Shops	1700 Wire Mill	2405 Coke Plant	1013 Steelmaking Shops[a]
1131 Sheet Mill	2421 Bessemer Mill	1489 Ensley	1131 Sheet Mill
1489 Ensley		1733 Pratt Car Shop	2122 Tin Mill
1700 Wire Mill		4203 Ore Processing	2210 Office & Clerical
1733 Pratt Car Shop			2927 Plant Protection
2122 Tin Mill			3662 Rail Transportation
2210 Office & Clerical			
2405 Coke Plant			
2927 Plant Protection			
3662 Rail Transportation			
4203 Ore Processing			
2421 Bessemer Mill			

SOURCE: E.B. Rich, Sub-District Director, USWA District #36.
a. Also includes pipe mill workers, some former coke plant workers, and any remaining maintenance workers. Included workers from plate mill shut down in 1979.

ity was reduced and the mining division eliminated. U.S. Steel continued to use the carrot of modernization to achieve concession in the 1970s.

David Roderick, in November 1979, expressed his opinion that Fairfield could be transformed into a profitable operation; but, along with this declaration of confidence in Fairfield came the announcement that the Fairfield Works wire mill would close, putting more than 100 additional employees out of work. Wire products were produced at a lower cost by foreign competitors and mini-mills. The closing of the plate mill was also made permanent.

Table 3.1
Fairfield Employment and Restructuring, 1955-1984

Month	Year	Employment	Type of restructuring
	1955	22,000	
	1960	20,000	
	1970	15,000	Iron ore mining discontinued
	1975	10,000	New Q-BOFs, Bessemer mill closed
July	1979	9,500	Remaining Ensley facilities closed
June	1980	3,000	Plate & wire mills closed, all hot-end shut down
December	1980	4,800	Number 8 blast furnace started up
January	1981	5,300	Ensley rail mill comes up
October	1981	3,800	Number 8 blast furnace shut down
November	1981	4,600	Number 7 blast furnace started up
April	1982	4,000	Coke battery shut down
June	1982	0	All hot- and finishing-end down
January	1984	2,400	Q-BOFs, blast furnaces, pipe mill all begin operation under the new December agreement

SOURCE: *Birmingham News*, various dates.

In May of 1980, discussion of the possible shutdown of the smaller Number 7 blast furnace became public, as did a large rollback in the ranks of management personnel. Approximately 70 management positions were affected, and there were reductions in pay and job classifications for a small number of assistants to division supervisors and a large number of general foremen. Management at USS had been reduced by 13,500 between 1980 and 1983.

Less than two weeks later, the official announcement came that the Number 7 furnace would be shut down, with the layoff of over 200 steelworkers; five days later, the company announced that an additional 700 steelworkers would be laid off due to production cutbacks resulting from an overall reduction in demand for steel. At the end of May, employment at Fairfield stood at approximately 6,000. The company announced that steel orders for the Fairfield facility were almost gone, and that a complete shutdown could become a reality within a few months. USS said that conditions had deteriorated to the point that the demand for Fairfield's steel had fallen to just 70,000 tons a month, which was only 58 percent of the 120,000 tons a month needed to break even.

Three days later, the news came from officials that Fairfield Works' large Number 8 blast furnace, the only furnace in operation, would shut down along with the Q-BOFs. All of the workforce would go on layoff, with the exception of those who would temporarily remain in the finishing end to work on inventories. This was the first complete shutdown in the facility's history.

On August 20, 1980, the smaller Number 7 blast furnace was designated to be put back into operation bringing approximately 700 employees back to work. The rationale given by management for the restart was a need to fill existing orders. Emphasis was placed on the fact that the demand for steel had not improved, and that the future was still very uncertain. Later that week, management and local USW officials disclosed that negotiations were underway to streamline the alleged inflexible Fairfield workforce into a competitive position. There were differences between plant management and union officials over how the streamlining would be done. To management, streamlining was necessary to reduce overhead and produce a profit, but for the employees, this meant the possible permanent loss of jobs. Privately, union officials admitted that some changes were needed and that they were "willing to work to improve efficiency, but not at the expense of work rules they had fought for and won over the years."

In 1981, USS added the carrot of building a new seamless-pipe mill and a continuous bloom caster. What it sought were concessions from the union and taxing agencies. The importance of modernization, from raw materials through the finishing process, is underscored by Crandall (1981) who maintains that efficiencies in steel production are realized only when all stages of the process have been modernized.

The roadblock to getting the pipe mill was removed on April 4, 1981, when USS and the USW reached a memorandum of understanding on changes in work rules at the Fairfield facility. The Pipe Mill Agreement called for changes in crew sizes, job duties, and work rules, and established new levels of man-hours in areas where hours were excessive. The pact called for no cuts in wages, benefits, or incentives and no consolidation of the numerous locals at Fairfield Works. The agreement had two components: a relinquishing of gains won in the arbitration of 15 grievances, and changes in manning practices. Comparisons had been made between manning practices at Fairfield Works, such as relief workers and helpers, and those at other USS facilities. The grievances given up by the union, with one exception, dealt with unilateral moves made by management in an effort to reduce manning levels in areas where it thought they were noncompetitive. Relief cranemen in two areas were eliminated, as well as helpers not used at other plants. Jobs, such as car repairman and laboratory utilityman, which were responsible for tasks no longer performed, or which were being performed elsewhere, were eliminated along with crew size arrangements which had been known to cause double-manning in some shifts.

However, a year after the Pipe Mill Agreement, the mill had not yet been built and the workforce had been reduced to just 4,000. The company continued to use shutdowns to pressure the union. It announced an extended total shutdown and hinted that it could become permanent, or at least last a long time, if some changes were not made. The union resisted wage concessions, but proposed other changes which could be made to cut costs. The steelworkers felt that the company wanted to lay off everybody and close down Fairfield until the starting of the pipe mill, a period of some 18 months.

In May, management announced a shutdown until early 1984 to pressure the union. Management had presented the USW district officers with a proposal to eliminate more than 100 jobs, as well as a number of changes in work rules. These changes were to involve the combining of jobs, assigning hourly work to supervisors, and the use of outside contractors to perform work normally done by union members. The proposal was rejected by the local presidents and chairmen in a unanimous vote. The union felt that the company had not made a commitment to keep Fairfield open, even if all of the concessions were met, since previous concessions had been followed by permanent layoffs. The union thought that the company wanted to use its refusal of concessions as an excuse to shut down Fairfield for 18 months until the pipe mill was ready. The union sought a promise in writing that USS would continue to keep Fairfield open if the union agreed to concessions. It pointed out that it had made concessions at the Ensley Rail Mill, and that the company had still moved its rail production to Gary, Indiana. The union was determined to make its position the bottom line. Under the concessions in the pipe mill agreement, the union had given up crew size grievances, many of which they had already won, and agreed to a "watering down" of an agreement that protected USW craftsmen while outside contractors were working in the plant. However, the complete shutdown occurred and laid-off steelworkers did not easily find new work in the Birmingham area. Prospective employers asked them to sign statements agreeing not to return to the mill, because Birmingham firms feared that former steelworkers would eventually return to their previous wage rates and excellent pension plans at USS. Prospective employers' fears were borne out in December of 1982, when USS announced that it would soon begin the processing of steelworkers' bids on the new jobs to be created by the pipe mill. These jobs would require extensive computer and technical training in such locations as Italy and Germany. Access to the jobs was based on seniority, experience, and the results of union-approved skill tests. Those with the longest seniority who were approaching retirement were expected to decline the pipe mill jobs because of the probability of losing large amounts of seniority.

Negotiations continued during the shutdown. USS sought to contract out maintenance previously performed by a central maintenance shop and offered to improve the hot-strip facilities and construct a new $100 million continuous slab caster which would require the employment of 1,600 workers.

Negotiations broke down in November 1983 and the union's district leadership went to the USW Executive Board in Pittsburgh and convinced it to pass a resolution which would prohibit local unions from entering into any local agreement which would violate the industry-wide master contract. The resolution of the Executive Board accused some steel companies of provoking "job wars" by trying to "force or entice" additional concessions by individual locals. The resolution was an attempt to prevent management from pitting one local against another in concessions. The USW Executive Board resolution, however, stopped short of forbidding work rule changes within the individual plants, and this became the key to the local agreement from the union; the site was kept open because the USW Executive Board allowed the district leadership to honor local agreements previously made with USX. The position of the local leadership was reported in the Birmingham News.

> We knew that U.S. Steel would go to the Mon Valley or to Lorain and cut a deal with them if we did not do something fast. They would have shopped around, and our twenty percent would have been zero. We did have a problem, however, because we then had to convince Lynn Williams to let us violate the resolution. We told him we had made prior commitments that we had to uphold, so he left it alone. (Rich 1988)

The local union presidents at Fairfield supported the district leadership, but the tradeoff advantage was very small. If maintenance was contracted out, 1,500 jobs would be lost in order to reemploy 1,600 members. Local negotiations had a deadline of December 27, when the USS board was to meet to announce the second phase of rationalization and additional plant closings.

Alabama Governor George Wallace mediated a settlement and on December 24, 1983, an agreement was reached allowing Fairfield Works to restart operations. The union had been convinced that the company would shut down the plant and take some of the equipment to its Gary plants if concessions were not made by the date of the Company's board meeting. Local union leaders initially played down the results of the agreement, claiming that the company had failed in its attempt to gain the major concessions that it once sought, but later evidence would show that the items contained in the "December Agreement" had cut very deeply. The agreement covered all present and future Fairfield Works facilities, and it had two major sections. In the first part of the agreement, there were "give backs" in work rules which had been won over the years, including drastic changes in Fairfield's maintenance shops. All work rules that were part of local agreements or that were part of mutual understandings would be eliminated. Rules governing such issues as crew size, manning levels, job assignments, hours of work, late starts, early quits, wash-up time, coffee breaks, lunch breaks, off days, and shift selection were discarded. A blanket statement was included to restrict any other practices not mentioned in the agreement that would hinder the future competitive operation of the Fairfield Works. According to Jerry Meyer of USS, "We tried at one time to do an inventory of the various 'arrangements' at Fairfield, but we couldn't get them all nailed down, so we put in the statement to cover ourselves for the ones we forgot."

The second part of the agreement related to maintenance employees. They were combined into plantwide shops to serve all of Fairfield Works from one location. Several maintenance shops had developed over the years with duplication of manpower. It was agreed that these shops, with the exception of line crews and the electronics shop, would be totally phased out through attrition. USS would, during and after attrition, reserve the right to contract out any work over and above the ability of the remaining maintenance personnel. This clause would result in the eventual loss of all but 85 of the 294 highly paid maintenance jobs at Fairfield. Also included in the agreement was a 35 percent cap on incentive payments, contracting out of 30 refuse and janitorial jobs.

In return for its concessions, the union was promised a continuous slab caster, which would be one of the most modern available, and it regained jobs for 1,600 steelworkers. The caster would require 200 to 300 fewer workers per day because of the elimination of the pouring, stripping, and reheating and rolling of ingots. Along with the caster would come improvements in hot-strip facilities.

Through restructuring the Pipe Mill Agreement and the December Agreement, the number of locals at Fairfield was reduced by half, from twelve to six (see figure 3.3). The new pipe mill employees and the centralized maintenance shops were both put into Local 1013, the largest of the Fairfield locals. Other locals had disappeared when Fairfield and Ensley facilities were closed. The Bessemer and wire mill locals disappeared as those facilities were closed, as did locals at the coking plant, the railroad car shop, ore conditioning lines, and the Ensley mills. Hoerr (1988) contends that because the Fairfield pact gave management great flexibility, it became the USS model for negotiating at other plants, but that the agreement was implemented without holding a ratification vote, and other locals felt the master agreements clause on manning was being abrogated. By the end of 1989 both the structure of the production process and labor-management relations had changed at Fairfield.[5]

Conclusions

Figure 3.4 presents a comparative summary of negotiations over downsizing in the adversarial countries. At Stelco, in Canada, where there was little restructuring, there was a stable and adversarial relationship in negotiations. The union was not involved in restructuring strategy, and bargaining focused on wages. Great Britain, on the other hand, presents, a mixed picture of both adversarial and cooperative situations. The steel unions, affiliated with the Labor party, were conservative and preferred not to strike. Because of this affiliation and the nationalization of steel, the unions as represented by the Trades Union Congress Steel Committee were brought into the restructuring early. In the 1970s, the relationship between the company and the unions was cooperative, with the Steel Committee accepting some closings and plant consolidations in return for keeping other plants open. Continued layoffs and plant closings, however, pitted the Steel Committee against the union branches at the individual sites that wanted to actively resist downsizing. The Steel Committee was also forced to alter its position from cooperative to adversarial by the BSC's strategy of negotiating worker reductions on a plant- by-plant basis. The severity of cuts and local resistance forced a long national strike in steel in 1980.

In the United States, there was a stable adversarial relationship between the steelworkers and the largest companies. Changes in market competition resulted in the breakup of multiemployer bargaining. At USS, the company sought concessions in manning and work practices from the locals. Locals were pitted against each other with the alternative of focusing on either plant closings or receiving new technology. The parties focused their negotiations on economic issues, and most of the companies settled quickly to keep their customers from

Figure 3.4
Comparative Bargaining in Adversarial Countries

| Countries | Environmental issues | | | | Outcomes | |
	Bargaining structure	Nature of relationship	Form of participation	Principal rules	Joint committees	Form of restructuring
Canada	Decentralized (pattern)	Adversarial	Negotiations	Wages	Yes	Wages
Great Britain	Centralized to decentralized	Cooperative to adversarial	Negotiations	Pensions	Yes	Employment adjustments
United States	Centralized (pattern) to decentralized	Adversarial	Negotiations	Pensions	No	Work rules, employment

going to overseas competitors. However, USS took a tougher stand, resulting in a lengthy strike in 1986. At the USS Fairfield, Alabama site, the company sought concessions in job classifications, contracting out and crew sizes. It threatened to close the site and withheld new technology, pending concessions from the locals. The union allowed the district to negotiate concessions and exceptions to the national agreement, which would not have been approved by the national bargaining committee.

The adjustment strategies used in Great Britain and the United States were: first, to stop hiring and allow normal attrition, quits, and retirements to reduce employment; second, to encourage voluntary early retirement; and third, to permanently lay off workers, but provide income supplements. The decentralized nature of collective bargaining in the United States limited the steelworkers' access to companies' decisionmaking process, and the breakup of industrywide bargaining resulted in pitting one company against another and one plant against another. The same events occurred in Great Britain; when BSC insisted on plant-by-plant negotiations, labor-shedding was negotiated locally, with the Steel Committee on occasion excluded from the table.

NOTES

1. Memorandum of Agreement Re Canada Works Consolidation Between Stelco, Inc. and Five Steelworkers Locals, April 27, 1984.

2. British Steel Corporation, Llanwern Works and the Trade Unions, *Memorandum of Understanding,* May 20, 1980.

3. Material in this section is taken from Brannen (1983) and Banks and Jones (1977).

4. Material for the Fairfield case study was obtained by David Williams from interviews with E.B. Rich, Director, USWA District 36, Howard Strevel, retired Director, USAW District 36, Jerry Meyer, General Manager, Arbitration and Labor Relations Administrator, USS, and reports in *The Birmingham News.*

5. In 1990, the federal government indicted and brought to trial USX and two United Steelworkers district officers on the charge that they conspired to negotiate the 1983 Fairfield agreement in return for receiving pension credits which allowed six union officers to begin receiving their pensions. In September 1990, USX was fined $4.1 million and the two Steelworkers officials were sentenced to jail. The sentences have been appealed. For an alternative view of the bargaining relationship, see Fischer (1990).

4
Collective Bargaining
in Cooperative Countries

This chapter discusses how the bargaining process and the relationship among employers, unions, and government affected restructuring in the cooperative countries. The expectation from the comparative systems matrix for the cooperative countries is that government would join employers and unions in bargaining, not just over the results of restructuring, but also over how restructuring would take place. Unions in these countries would be expected to facilitate adjustment and reduce the costs of restructuring.

The cooperative countries also have other forms of employee participation. Works councils in Belgium, Luxemburg, Germany, and Sweden are the result of codetermination legislation. The essential features of the institutional arrangement are often works councils, workers' representatives on the supervisory boards of companies, and labor directors on their management boards. The central institution is the works council in every establishment elected by all the workers, whether they are union members or not. Works councils are primarily consultative, except in Germany where they may also be co-decisionmakers, receive information, or negotiate. The unions have extended their influence to the shop-floor level by running union members for plant works councils. The expected effect of works councils on restructuring is not clear. It could be argued either that joint decisionmaking raises costs by causing delays and expensive adjustment programs, or that works councils assist restructuring by increasing worker cooperation.

Belgium and Luxembourg

Collective bargaining in Belgium is a multitiered process. It can take place at the national, regional or company level. Since 1975, there have been few national agreements. What does exist is a combination of national consultations and multiemployer bargaining. Two forms of consultation are the National Labor Council and Joint Parity Committee for each sector. The National Labor Council proposes general agreements on such issues as: part-time work (1981), the hiring and selection of new employees (1983) and the introduction of new technology (1983). The Joint Parity Committees can also negotiate contracts and propose company settlements. However, the usual forms of negotiation are either between employer associations and unions by industrial sector on a regional basis, usually for one year, or at the company level, usually for two years. Workers are covered by both national agreements and local contracts. National agreements cover broad issues such as technological change, while local agreements cover wages and hours.[1]

About 70 percent of the population is organized, with the unions affiliated with one of the confederations. The major confederations are divided along political lines, each supporting either the Christian or Socialist parties. The Christian Trade Union Confederation is strongest in the north, and the General Belgium Labor Federation is strongest in the south. The Christian Trade Union Confederation's metal trade union claimed 231,551 members in 1982, and the Belgium Labor Federation claimed 211,289 in 1980 (Blanpain 1984).

Exclusive jurisdiction does not exist in Belgium, and competition between the two metal trade unions is strong, particularly at the plant level. Employee representation at the plant level is provided by three groups: the union delegation, the works council, and the Committee for Health and Safety. The unions indirectly control these other forms of employee representation, either by directly appointing the union delegates to the Health and Safety Committee or having exclusive rights to nominate the works council.

Employer associations and individual companies both negotiate contracts in Belgium. The major employer association in Belgium is the Federation of Belgium Enterprises, which is composed of 39 sectoral associations covering 35,000 companies. It represents about 75 percent of the companies employing more than 10 workers. The employer association in the metal industry is Fabrimetal. In collective bargaining, it is organized on a regional basis to either assist employers or to directly negotiate regional contracts (Windmuller and Gladstone 1984).

Belgium steelworkers protested restructuring more actively than steelworkers in the other seven countries. Each new restructuring plan brought opposition from the unions in the form of strikes and demonstrations (Capron 1986). Reductions in employment projected by the Claes Plan of 1978-80 were sharply scaled down from 4,675 to 1,380 because of union resistence. Table 4.1 shows the employment reductions first proposed by the government and the final agreement after union resistance. The basis of both the blue-collar and white-collar agreements, which included early pensions and hours of work, was a report by the McKinsey consulting firm. McKinsey has played a major role in steel restructuring around the world because its recommendations for downsizing based on international performance standards have been widely applied.

Table 4.1
Reductions in Employment Under the Claes Plans

Company	First agreement	Final agreement
Boel	0	0
Clabecq	650	10 - 60
Fabrifer	60 - 75	0
Charleroi	2,300 - 2,800	600 - 650
Leige	700 - 1,150	500 - 600
Phenix	0	50
Sidmar	0	0
Usines aTubes de la mense		20
Possible maximum reduction	4,675	1,380

In the first half of 1982, the Belgium steel unions protested at both the European Economic Community (EEC) offices in Brussels and in the steel towns. In February and March, they protested in Brussels, and the government was concerned that the demonstrations would lead to longer strikes in the steel towns of Wallonia. The workers there had engaged in a number of short strikes in March and April to protest the austerity policy of the Martens V government and its plans to close the plants of Liege and Charleroi. The Social-Christian participation in the Martens cabinet placed that party in Wallonia in a difficult position. It had to decide whether to support the Belgium Labor Federation strikes or its own government. By the end of March, the Christian Trade Union Confederation decided to condemn the multiple strike actions and follow the national line which broke the common union front.

The Gandois Plan of 1983, discussed in chapter 2, was also resisted at the local level, rather than by the national federation, when workers in the steel towns where Cockerill-Sambre had plants demonstrated. This is similar to the British and U.S. cases, where the greatest resistance was at the local rather than national level. The intensity of resistance by each of the union confederations depended upon its political alignment with either the party in office (Catholic-Liberal) or the party out of office (Socialist), as well as its strength in the regions. Resistance to the Gandois Plan was strongest in the Metalworking Union, the Belgium Labor Federation affiliate which supported the Socialist party. The Christian Workers Union of the Christian Trade Union Confederation was reluctant to strike, since it supported the Catholic-Liberal coalition which had helped develop the restructuring plan. The May 1983 contact, which called for an overall decrease in wages of between 5 and 10 percent, was rejected. The Martens V government had taken the position that, since Cockerill-Sambre was benefiting from public aid, the workers should make a contribution towards restoring the company's competitiveness by accepting a wage reduction. It put pressure on the unions and management by withholding aid to cover the company's short-term cash drain. Resistance from the metalworkers appeared to be less over steel restructuring and more over the loss of wage indexation. The government was forced to withdraw its idea of submitting the plan to a vote by the workers. Restructuring in steel was resisted through the spring of 1984 because it coincided with the institution of austerity wage programs in both Belgium and Luxembourg.

The metalworkers unions from the Belgium Labor Federation and Christian Trade Union Confederation contested elections at Sidmar. The Labor Federation protested wage freezes and plant closings, and succeeded in increasing representation at Sidmar between 1967 and 1979 (Van Den Hof 1984). The economic regulations of the works council at Sidmar detailed its organization as well as the information it was to receive about the firm's competitive position, production figures, finances, personnel costs, budget, future, plans, and research expenditures.

Luxembourg employs the concept of "social partnership" in labor-management relations with comprehensive conciliation arrangements. About 70 percent of the workers are covered by contracts, and negotiations take place either at the sectoral level or at the company level as at Arbed. The unions are divided along religious and political lines. The principal federations are the Socialist Confederation with 33,000 blue- and white-collar members, the Socialist-Christian Confederation with 15,000 members, and the nonaligned private-sector white-collar organization with 15,000 members. On the employers' side, the principal association is the Federation des Industriels Luxembourgeois, which provides guidance but does not directly engage in collective bargaining.

Unions and employers are represented on a number of joint and tripartite committees such as the National Economic and Social Council, the Employment Supervisory Board, the Steel Tripartite and General Tripartite Commissions. Six statute-based occupational chambers representing different industries and employees (private, manual, nonmanual, and public) are consulted on all legislation affecting their members.

The conciliation system was reinforced in a tripartite conference in 1977, which set as its objectives the prevention of unemployment, maintenance of social peace, helping the steel industry recover, and softening social consequences and human suffering due to the economic crisis. A steel tripartite conference was also established, which called for a reduction in the steel labor force by 31 percent between 1974 and 1979 (from 29,000 to 20,000 workers), with expectations of a 43 percent drop in steelworkers over 10 years to 16,500. The programs that aided this transition are discussed in chapter 5.

There has been tripartite cooperation in the matter of restructuring. The 1981 agreement in steel said, "The signatories recognize the need for technological progress. They are aware of the fact that rationalization and modernization lead to changes in the employment structure which may result in transfers and displacement" (Committee on Tripartite Coordination 1981, p. 3). The same agreement provides for wage guarantees for the workers affected by such changes. The agreement also states that, in view of the strained economic and financial situation of the companies, the trade unions do not demand a general wage increase or a general reduction in hours of work. This commitment would cease if there was considerable improvement in steel production. The agreement called for a 3 percent increase in white-collar salaries and no increase in blue-collar wages for 1981-1983, the establishment of an anticrisis division for laid-off workers rescinding the automatic cost-of-living increase of 1.5 percent, and delaying the cost-of-living adjustments by one month.

There are three forms of employee participation in Luxembourg. Worker committees engage in dialogue about employee matters relating to working conditions, job security, and social legislation. These committees are required in companies with more than 1500 employees. There is also the Joint Works Council, which is an advisory body in major decisions related to investment in plant, manufacturing process, or working conditions. These are required in plants with 150 or more employees. Finally, there are employee representatives on management boards. Representatives of the workers and trade unions occupy one-third of the seats on the board of directors of iron and steel companies. There are continuous negotiations during restructuring between management and the worker committees in steel.

Germany

Collective bargaining in Germany is conducted between employer associations and the unions on a geographical basis. Contracts are negotiated that cover a single state (Lander) or part of a state. The employer associations are composed of firms in a number of related industries and represent both large and small employers with different competitive conditions. For example, the metals industry covers autos and electrical equipment, as well as steel. There are two separate employer associations: one for iron and steel and one for metalworking. The logic for this separation is that in iron and steel, the labor director, who is often a former union member, sits on the corporation's supervisory board; this could result in a union member representing the employer association. In steel, the labor director has often come out of the union, since codetermination requires approval of this position by the employee representatives on the managing board of the company. The union counterpart to the employer association is IG Metall, the largest German union. Unions are not only strong participants in collective bargaining, but they have exerted considerable influence on political and social life. Some of the unions' strength comes from their role in institutionalized participation in codetermination. Codetermination provides for employee representation at the plant and company levels and will be discussed later in this section.

A typical IG Metall negotiation starts when goals are discussed among union members at the plant level, which makes recommendations to the union. The union then informs the company of its position before termination of the contact. Next, a negotiating committee is established, and bargaining starts two weeks before the expiration date. No strike or lockout may occur until four weeks after the expiration date of the contract. Unions do not have exclusive jurisdiction in Germany, as they do in the United States, and several unions may represent the workers in a plant. In practice, IG Metall has the largest membership and maintains offices to service its members and larger districts, and local offices are located near large plants. Isolated plants with a small number of union members are provided with fewer services. Since negotiations at the plant level are conducted by the works council, the unions have developed informal arrangements at the shopfloor level to maintain worker loyalty. The unions have shop stewards or *vertrauensleute* (men and women of confidence) to whom members can go for an informal solution to grievances. The *vertrauensleute* in the plant may be appointed by the union or elected by the organized employees of the plant. These union representatives are the communications link between union members and the union. If the shop steward cannot settle the grievance informally, then it goes to the works council. The metalworkers maintain ties to the works councils by offering technical services on such issues as the setting of wage rates and the timing of line speeds and conduct training sessions. Finally, the union may be represented on the supervisory board of the steel companies through full-time union officers who have been elected by the employees under codetermination. Information reaches the union from the plant through its members on the works council and its shop stewards.

The role of collective bargaining in German steel restructuring can be understood within the context of a labor movement that cooperated in German economic development after the Second World War. The Social Democratic party dominated parliament, and it was expected to guarantee a risk-free capitalist economy along with government planning and codetermination. Among the social partnership's greatest successes were the establishment of codetermination in steel and coal in 1951, and its extension in a different form to other firms. In the Co-Determination Act of 1951, workers' representatives were included in the company structure. Parity in workers' representation (five workers and five shareholders' representatives, with a neutral eleventh member) was prescribed for supervisory boards. The shareholders elect the supervisory board, which designates the management board. In the steel and coal industry, management boards must include a "labor director" who can be appointed or dismissed only with the consent of the majority of the workers' members on the supervisory board.

IG Metall and the employers had a relatively peaceful partnership during restructuring. The union accepted the need for implementing layoffs, but pressed for early retirement rather than discharges. It also sought layoffs concentrated in groups with low conflict potential and high compensation to soften the impact. Esser and Vath (1986) argue that IG Metall had in mind a priority list of workers who were to be defended. They maintain that from the most to the least protected, the thinking was: most efficient workers, other workers, the young, the unemployed, and finally foreign workers. IG Metall, particularly in the Saar, was able to keep the number of direct dismissals low. There is a consensus in Germany that codetermination in steel made a substantial contribution to the general climate of cooperation and industrial peace in steel. However, scholars differ in their views of the effects of codetermination on steel restructuring, and these are discussed later in this section.

The overall agreement for workforce changes was drafted first in 1975 and updated in 1978; discussions included unions and the works councils. The issue arose concerning whether the union should be included in discussions concerning workforce reductions, which is a topic where works council participation is required. Political pressure was exerted to include the unions. Disputes also occurred among the works councils in multiplant firms. The works councils at the three major Thyssen locations had different interests. The works councils in the two plants facing the largest cutbacks sought to insure the maintenance of jobs for their members. The deputy director of IG Metall was also a member of the supervisory board of Thyssen, and the unions took an active role in discussions about employment reductions.

The cases of Hoesch and Krupp are additional examples of how the unions and works councils used their political power to effect restructuring. Estel, the holding company formed by Hoesch and Hoogovens, faced a reduction in demand. In February 1980, the first social plan was agreed to between the firm and its works council under which the workforce was reduced by 2,000. (Social plans will be discussed in chapter 5.) In the implementation of the plan, the estimate of job loss ran from 4,000 to 10,000. Hoesch requested a federal subsidy to help build a new plant, and both the works councils and IG Metall pressured the federal government and the state government of North-Rhine Westphalia to assist with a low-interest loan. When Estel decided to scrap its plans for a new plant, union members felt sold out by the company. A number of strikes took place, and 15,000 Hoesch workers at two plants went on strike on October 31, 1980 and demonstrated outside the company's offices. These worker-led demonstrations were similar to those carried out by union members rather than their union leaders in Britain and Belgium.

At a Dortmund Conference in December 1980, the works council in Estel accepted a new social plan with less favorable conditions and the possibility of dismissals. The works councils and the unions faced the same conditions as their counterparts in Britain who had been told to accept employment reductions at established sites or face the possibility of plant closings and the development of new sites. The unions and works councils in Germany, however, in accepting these reductions, also accepted a share of the responsibility.

The strength of the metalworkers is evident from their ability to block the first restructuring plan of Hoesch and Krupp to form one company. This plan was proposed by the federal government, but blocked at the state level, and a new plan developed with worker consultation was substituted. In May 1981, IG Metall proposed that the restructuring of the steel industry must not lead to new overcapacity; plants must not be shut down before replacement jobs are available in the neighborhood; diversification in the Ruhr should be combined with the diversification of individual steel firms; there should be cuts in working time; and finally, restructuring should require the participation of the works councils and trade unions. The recent union efforts have been aimed at reducing the workweek in order to preserve jobs.

Steel and coal mining were the first industries to come under codetermination in Germany through the Works Constitution Act of 1951 and the Works Constitution Act of 1952 (Streeck 1984). Works councils and unions have separate jurisdictions. The unions negotiate annual contracts covering wages, while works council approval is required in setting work time, temporary short time, overtime work, piece rates, pay systems, suggestion schemes, holiday schedules, monitoring of performance, wages above the negotiated rate, and the work environment. They must also be consulted in personnel selection and training, holiday and vacation pay, selecting of wage rates for new jobs, and the reevaluation of pay when employees are transferred between jobs. Consultation with the works council is required for technological change. Although works council members are frequently union members, the two are formally separate organizations. The union is represented at the plant level by shop stewards. The Hamborn plant of Thyssen in Duisberg, with 21,000 employees in 1982, also had four works council committees: wage and salary, work time, health and safety, and social.

Worker participation on the supervisory board is another vehicle for implementing codetermination. The supervisory board of steel firms is composed of an equal number of representatives elected by the shareholders and the employees, with an additional neutral member. The shareholders elect five, the union appoints three, and the employees elect two members. A second board, the management board, is responsible for the daily operations of the company and is similar to the U.S. firm's executive committee. None of the management board members are on the supervisory board. The industrial relations vice-president or labor director (arbeitsdirektor) serves on the management board. In the steel industry, the labor director serves at the pleasure of the workforce and has the approval of the union, while in other industries, such as autos, the labor director's appointment and responsibilities are clearly received from management. In a multiplant firm, a member of the plant works council serves on the company works council, and the chairman of the works council also serves as deputy chairman of the supervisory board.

There is a difference in opinion concerning how well the works councils represent employees' interests, and how much information is shared by management (Altmann 1984). In large multiplant companies, plant works councils appear to be quite removed from the shop floor. Works council chairmen under these conditions get their information about shop-floor sentiments from the shop stewards. The works council members are often former line workers, and they may be at a disadvantage in negotiations with management, particularly on matters that require technical knowledge and scientific skills, such as the introduction of new processes. The Duisberg steel area has held a series of joint study groups for the works councils of the steel companies and the shop stewards to discuss rationalization and technological change. Works councils often have to rely on union experts who are few in number and not available for the smaller companies.

Diversification of the steel firms into other products has resulted in steel declining to a minority percentage of some of the companies' business, and the question has come up whether steel firms are still covered by the 1951 legislation. Firms that diversify out of steel can switch out of the 1951 to the 1972 legislation under which workers have less influence on the supervisory boards. However, when Mannesman sought to reorganize in 1972 to escape the 1951 Law, the reorganization was not allowed and was opposed by the unions and the Social Democrats. This switch was again blocked by the unions in 1981-82.

The unions and works councils have reacted to economic restructuring and technological change at three levels: politics, collective bargaining, and codetermination. IG Metall has been most successful in affecting the pace of economic restructuring through the political process. It has been able to prevent the closing of plants and the shifting of production by the use of its political strength, and companies have backed down from their plans when faced with political opposition. The German Labor Federation successfully opposed the restructuring of steel into two divisions. At the national level, there have been few guidelines for restructuring, and both Socialist and Conservative governments have refrained from interfering in the codetermination process.

Restructuring has proceeded at both the industry level and the plant level, and the activities of the unions and works councils have overlapped. Negotiations at the industry level have focused on wages and reduction of the hours of work. The trade union objective is the 35-hour week. The unions have agreed that a reduction in working time would maintain and even increase the number of jobs. This argument has been strongly rejected by the employers. In 1984, a long strike affecting the metal industry ended in an agreement on the introduction of the 38 1/2-hour week. A refinement of this principle was achieved in the industrywide metals agreement in October 1984, which provided for a 38-hour week. IG Metall has argued that this reduction of working time affected job security by saving 7,000 jobs. However, the employers disagreed and point out that opinion polls among steelworkers show that they prefer early retirement to a further reduction of the weekly working time. Workweek reductions have been negotiated three times, and the 35-hour week will begin 1995.

There has been no industrywide negotiated agreement on workforce reductions. Negotiations at the company level with the union and at the plant level with the works council have focused on workforce reductions. Public policy requires management to consult the works council over reductions of operations, closure of the whole establishment or significant departments, as well as significant changes in the organization, purpose, or plan of the establishment, and the introduction of entirely new work methods and production processes. In law and practice, works councils are closely associated with decisions about termination of employment and measures to avoid or mitigate the effects of dismissals. In 1974-75, the works council and state government were able to prevent a plant closing and forced the company to reduce employment at all of its facilities rather than at a single site.

The works council and management must also negotiate a "social plan" if there is to be a layoff of 100 or more workers or a plant closing. This plan often provides for compensation to workers whose employment is terminated. Social plans have been negotiated in all of the steel companies, and some examples are presented in chapter 5. Plans vary, but will often include reductions in work time (with some form of financial compensation for the ensuing loss of earnings), special payments in addition to public unemployment benefits, old-age pensions for those who accept early retirement, and various forms of severance pay. Social plans supplement the benefits which workers have received from the EEC, as well as those to which they are entitled under statutory unemployment benefit programs and old-age pension programs.

At Bohler, a small steel company, a social plan was negotiated in 1981 because of the reduction of 880 workers at its Dusseldorf plant (Lehnek 1982). The social plan was in force until all claims over work reductions were settled. Reductions were accomplished by early retirement, transfers, and dismissals. Those over 57 were eligible for retirement. Transfers to other plants were negotiated for those 40 years of age with 25 years of service or 50 years of age with 10 years of service. Those who faced dismissal received severance pay based on age, seniority and pay level. The average dismissal payment was $4,425. The Bohler plan required that workers transferred be matched with new jobs based on their qualifications or their ability to be retrained after no more than a six-week program. For a worker who was offered a job and refused it for a lower-paying job, the higher-paying job offered was considered the wage guaranty basis.

There are two positions with regard to the effects of codetermination on steel restructuring in Germany. Thimm (1980; 1987) represents the position that works councils made change more difficult, and Thelen (1987) represents the position that codetermination assisted in the cooperative climate.

Thimm examined the impact of codetermination on restructuring at Arbed-Saarstahl in the 1980s. Arbed-Saarstahl was the result of a merger and restructuring subsidies from Luxembourg and the German State of Saarland. Marginal plants were to be closed. In this case, management needed the union representatives on the supervisory board to assist them in gaining the support of IG Metall and the Social-Democratic legislators in order to obtain subsidies. Thimm argues that the company could not have survived without these subsidies, and that the high cost of layoffs undermined the financial stability of the company and absorbed potential investment funds. Codetermination, he says, provided a formal structure and justification for delaying the hard decisions of restructuring by searching for consensus. Further, he contends that labor's influence through codetermination created rigidities, especially in wages and employment, and that made successful adaptation and economic change more difficult. Codetermination encouraged the formation of a coalition of local labor representatives, steel managers, and regional politicians to stall or block adjustment. Together they lobbied for state assistance, which delayed restructuring.

Thimm appears to contradict himself when he argues that the strength of German steel is due to union and works council support of investment policies during the 1970s. Up to 1978, codetermination helped the transition. After that, government became more important in the adjustment process. Thimm concludes that codetermination has *not* had a negative effect on the major German steel companies, and points out that with the exception of 1975-1977 or 1981-1987, German steel has remained profitable.

Thelen, on the other hand, argues that German steel responded effectively and peacefully in the marketplace and with regard to industrial conflict and labor participation. Adjustment has been consensual and less disruptive in Germany, and codetermination has provided the institutional framework for achieving the political settlement necessary for successful adjustment. She concludes that codetermination shifted managers' attention from quick fixes to long-term solutions by causing joint discussions. At a relatively early stage, labor was brought in to discuss who was to bear how much of the cost of adjustment, and codetermination offered a forum for the political conflicts that accompanied economic change. Thelen's evidence is that, since 1974, German steel has shed 40 percent of its workforce without national unrest and without mass layoffs, through early retirement and voluntary severance schemes.

In a rebuttal to Thimm, Thelen pointed out that Arbed-Saarstahl is an exception. It is Germany's most subsidized steel firm, receiving subsidies from the government from 1980 to 1985 that equalled all other German steel producers combined. For the other firms, government support was explicitly tied to restructuring plans that would result in capacity reductions. She pointed out that while Thyssen and Krupp moved to change their technology and product mix, U.S. and French firms developed coalitions for protection and subsidies.

Thelen also argues that wage and employment flexibility may not be what firms have to seek in order to make them more competitive. That is, the systems that emphasize sharp reductions in wages and levels of employment may not become most competitive. Rather, an examination of comparable plants in Britain, Sweden and the Netherlands indicated that the two main sources of productivity advantage for the plants was through capacity utilization and the organization of labor. Maintenance flexibility was crucial, and versatility became important. She argues that the flexibility of American managers in regard to wages and employment may provide a superficial flexibility through short-term relief without facing the more fundamental sources of competitive difficulties. On the other hand, German managers have to assume a longer term perspective.

Schroter (1986) presented another example of the role of codetermination in German steel restructuring. He traced the history of Hoesch in Dortmund, and reported that in 1979, when management presented a new strategy of allowing steel production in Dortmund to stagnate, concentrating at one site and reducing the number of employees without dismissals, the workers' answer was that no further agreement would be given to rationalization and reduction of employment without a comprehensive plan. The union at the plant demanded that no further reduction of jobs be made without creating alternative jobs to compensate for lost workplaces. However, the workers' representatives at the shop floor and on the board and the works council could not agree on this demand. In 1979, the workers' demand moved from the company to the regional government, and a demonstration was held in Dortmund in November 1980. Hoesch's problems were no longer internal, and a plan was agreed to by government, management, and the workers to build a new plant and reduce jobs by 4,200. This was tied to a state commitment for assistance in the form of a loan and no dismissals. Reductions were to be accomplished by unemployment grants, firm subsidies, early retirement, and normal attrition.

Japan

Collective bargaining in Japan is generally conducted at the company or plant level between a company union and management. A typical multiplant firm bargains with labor at the company level, the plant level, and at subdivisions within each plant (Levine 1981). At the company level, agreements are reached on general working conditions, such as working hours, wages, and conditions of employment, union activity including the number of full-time union officials and their treatment, and grievance procedures. At the plant level, agreements are reached on local grievance and joint consultation procedures, the number of full-time union officials at the plant level, union use of company facilities, and application of companywide rules, such as working hours. At the plant subdivision level, agreements are reached on application of company- and plant-level agreement (Kozo 1984). Wage negotiations are conducted in the spring and bonus negotiations in the summer and winter.

At Nippon Steel Corporation (NSC), discussions between labor and management are conducted according to the labor agreement, and minutes of the meetings are prepared for all discussions (Abe 1989). In addition to these formal discussions, informal discussions and exchanges are used to inform the union of company policies and obtain the union's opinion. The labor agreement stipulates that, "The company shall discuss matters common to all the company with the federation at the head office and matters concerned with each worker with the union at the works."[2]

The structure of collective bargaining at NSC is divided into three levels: headquarters, individual works, and individual plant. At the headquarters and works levels, collective bargaining is carried out through the management council and the labor-management committee. Collective bargaining covers wages and the contract. The management council functions as a forum for the transmission of information. It meets on a quarterly basis at the headquarters level and gives the union information on managements policies, the balance sheet, and production plans. At the works level, it gives the union information on production, the installation of new technology, and possible shutdowns. The labor-management committee both negotiates and transmits information. It meets as the occasion demands at the headquarters level and twice a month at the works level. Among the topics discussed are changes in personnel, employee housing, and monthly production plans.

The shop-floor level has a joint production committee composed of the superintendent and 10 management members, and the union local's chair and nine union members. They meet once a month to trade information on production, technology, shutdowns, and sales.

Spring wage negotiations are held between NSC and the trade union federation. The federation is made up of 12 unions, each of which has locals in the plants. Negotiations over personnel reductions occur at the works level through the joint labor-management committee composed of the general manager and the officers of the local union. The local union officers report to the local chapters and receive the responses of the members from the local chapters.

Sweden

Collective bargaining for blue-collar workers follows a three-stage format. The first stage is the frame agreements or branch agreements. The Swedish Employers Confederation and the Swedish Trade Unions Confederation negotiate economywide standards as a floor for compensation, which includes pay increases, "wage-drift" differentials for affected groups, supplemental pay provisions for classes of workers receiving low pay, overtime rates, rules regarding shift work, and normal workweek hours. At the second stage, employer associations affiliated with the Employers Confederation and trade unions affiliated with the Trade Unions Confederation use the frame agreement to conclude a contract at the sector level. Subjects include hours of work, shift work, and overtime pay. The provisions in the economywide agreement have usually served as minimum standards for sector trade unions, which attempt to negotiate additions. The Swedish Steel Corporation (SSAB) is not part of the Employers Confederation, since it is considered a public-sector company and public-sector companies have their own confederation. The third, or local, stage negotiates over issues such as safety or the introduction of new technology and the distribution of the money. Union affiliates of the Central Organization of Salaried Employees follow a somewhat different three-stage process.

Approximately 90 percent of all blue-collar workers and 80 percent of all white-collar workers are organized (European Trade Union Institute 1983). The metalworkers union (Metall) was the largest national trade union in the Trade Unions Confederation, but lost its position to the municipal workers union with the growth in the public sector. In

1983, decentralized bargaining became the norm when the engineering employers association insisted on separate negotiations with Metall.[3]

The Employee Participation in Decision Making Act of 1977 gave unions the authority to operate at the strategy level of restructuring. The Act replaced former agreements over works councils and extended coverage beyond the former 25 employee minimum to all companies with one or more union employees. The Act was broad and could be interpreted to cover almost any workplace activity; it clearly placed the unions in a central role, since it required negotiation over important changes and guaranteed a level of employee participation in decision-making which exceeded the unions' role through collective bargaining. Under the legislation, the employers were obliged to provide information to the trade unions, on their initiative, concerning production, finance, and employment policy.

The basis of labor-management relations in Sweden is the Employee Participation in Decision Making Act and the 1982 agreements between the Trade Unions Confederation, the Federation of Salaried Employees, and the Employers Confederation. Both were to be operationalized at the local level, but this has created a problem for the unions. Gospel (1983) concluded that in Sweden, unions are particularly well developed and powerful at the national level; however, plant-level organization is relatively underdeveloped, certainly in comparison to shop steward committees in Britain and union locals in the United States. Companywide union organization is even more limited in Sweden. The implication is that there exists a mismatch in sophistication between the unions and management at the two levels of decisionmaking. The unions have the sophistication at the national level but not at the company and shop-floor levels. Since the first agreement under the Employee Participation in Decision Making Act, the unions have focused on the issue of getting the companies to pay for consultants for the union to help them at the company and local levels in the analysis and interpretation of information relevant to decisionmaking. This was done at SSAB. They have also requested employer-sponsored education programs for union members on company boards of directors.

Another issue of union participation is the timing with which information is made available to the union. From the union point of view, the recognition and sorting of alternatives in a decisionmaking situation is just as important as having a voice in choosing which of the final alternatives is implemented. The common complaint among unions is that they are not required to be included in this initial sorting of alternatives, and when they are brought into the process, the information provided by the employer is focused only on those alternatives that have survived the employer's unilateral decision. Labor court rulings (1978-1980) determined that the employees had the right to investigate alternatives prior to negotiation.

The merger of Sweden's three major steel companies into SSAB provided the first national opportunity to test the impact of the codetermination legislation of 1977 on corporate policy and strategy (Hedberg 1979). Labor-management relations had been different in each of the three companies. Domnarvet, owned by Stora, was the largest steelworks in Scandinavia. It had a tradition as a research-oriented multipurpose steelmaker, which had engaged in an ambitious investment program in the early 1970s with a new, wide-rolling mill. The trade unions in this company were strong, with an emphasis on traditional collective bargaining and wage negotiations. There was little cooperation between the white- and blue-collar unions. Lulea, owned by Norrbottens Jarnverk AB, was a multipurpose factory complex which had suffered continued losses and quality problems. The unions were strong at this site and had used their political connections to gain continued government support for the steelworks. Oxelösund, owned by Granges, specialized in heavy steel plates for ships. The site had a progressive management and close cooperation among its unions (Bain 1987a).

The blue- and white-collar labor federations asked for representation at the outset on the government commission that was to produce a corporate strategy. The unions also formed a task force and study group, which would be available to independently evaluate the commission's work. When serious negotiations among the three firms developed in the spring and summer of 1977, Oxelösund sent a delegation that had both management and union representatives. This set the tone for future negotiations, and both management and union representatives from each of the three companies were present at negotiations. The union representatives requested a task force of employees from all of the affected units, including steel, mining, and railroads; they also called in a consultant, Allan Larsson, who represented the unions during negotiations. In return for their role at the strategy level, the unions used their political power to push for government loans that would guarantee the continuance of the new company with the purchase of private property, patents, and equipment (Larsson 1986).

Bjorn Wahlstrom, president of the new company, presented a plan in November 1977 that was based on the work of the three joint committees. These joint committees had both union and management representatives, and the union's participation in the development of this plan appeared to commit them to Wahlstrom's proposal. The unions resisted acceptance of Wahlstrom's plan, however. They felt that worker input and codetermination had been shunted off to a number of internal boards with no power, and a compromise was reached by the creation of a joint union-management interim organization to handle the transition for six months (Nyquist 1986). The unions needed this time in order to deal with their internal problems. The blue-collar and white-collar labor federations had negotiated separately and needed time to study the issues and implications of the merger and to establish a joint union strategy. They had to establish a strong united front made up of the different unions and separate production sites, develop a role for the union representatives in the decision bodies at each site, and allow a large number of union representatives to be exposed to SSAB's problems.

The unions represented a much broader constituency with a political agenda, while management was more homogeneous and was represented at the top by the new company's president and vice-presidents. The vice-presidents each participated in one or more of the division management groups. At the plant level, management was already in place. The unions, on the other hand, had never coordinated their activities among the three companies and in some cases not amongst themselves at each steel site. The employees in the steel works belonged to the metalworkers unions. These unions were coordinated by the Trade Unions Confederation. The white-collar workers cooperated under the national bargaining umbrella of the Federation of Salaried Employees and were represented by three different unions: one for the first-line supervisors, one for the white-collar employees, and one for the civil engineers. The mine workers were also part of the Trade Unions Confederation, and the railroad company had both blue- and white-collar unions.

The unions, instead of waiting for a plan that they would then have to negotiate issue by issue, wanted to be part of an interim organization that would develop the overall strategy for restructuring. The principal aspects of the arrangement arrived at in the fall of 1977 were that the unions were committed from the beginning to the merger and restructuring and had already approved of the idea. The unions' commitment was reinforced by their involvement in lobbying for government support for the loan guarantees. The difficult problem of deciding which facilities would be shut down and which would receive new investment was postponed by the creation of the joint interim organization, which would deal with the issues through a number of working groups.

The joint interim merger organization was composed of the central project management group, which included top management and union representatives from the different trades and units. There were also eight central project groups, each in a different functional area with both union and management representatives. The central project groups represented one place that the information and negotiation aspects of codetermination were carried out. Finally, local project groups coordinated the activities at the three major sites. As the discussions continued, an additional layer—the Division Management Groups—with both management and union representatives, was added. These division groups would later form the basis for the permanent new divisions in SSAB.

Allan Larsson and a research team from the Swedish Center for Working Life assisted the unions. The research team consisted of three members who were already involved in the central project groups, while others took a support role and engaged in special studies requested by the unions. Between project group meetings, the union representatives, Allan Larsson, and the Working Life team met to evaluate the issues and frame their own amendments and positions.

Negotiations proceeded at the national and local levels. Economic, market, and technological strategies were set at the national level, while the locals negotiated over how restructuring would take place, particularly how the workforce would be affected. Early in 1978, the more than 200 union representatives on the major committees and task forces determined that they were unfamiliar with the merger process and hadn't formed a cohesive position on many of the issues, and they asked for additional time beyond the six months to consider all of the issues. The union representatives opposed early retirement in the first plan, threatening to submit everything to formal negotiations if they were not given an extension, and they were.

The Employee Participation in Decision Making Act of 1977 placed considerable emphasis on the local union, which explains why bargaining over restructuring was carried out at the three sites and why separate local agreements were negotiated. The steel plants were extremely important to the economic health of each of the communities. Table 4.2 presents employment at the SSAB plant in Oxelösund relative to the city.

Table 4.2
Oxelösund City and Plant Employment, 1957-1983

	Year				
	1957	1962	1978	1979	1983
Population of city	6,000	12,000	14,000	14,000	14,000
Employment at plant	800	3,000	3,700	3,890	3,119
Plant as a percentage of city	13.3	25	26.4	27.8	22.2

SOURCE: SSAB, Oxelösund facility.

Internal union problems developed among the three locations and between the unions at each site. At the local level, the unions defended their own site as a viable production unit and as a site to maintain overall employment within the larger plan. The sites were in competition with each other over where the cutbacks would take place and where new technology would be installed. The mining towns in central Sweden particularly would suffer if the production of raw steel was eliminated at Lulea, the central steel site; on the other hand, if Domnarvet lost its raw steel production, it would lose jobs, including jobs in the surrounding mining district. The unions were pressured to use their influence at the national political level to gain government help for the mining towns. The locals and the national unions had to work together in a unified front to press for companywide solutions to labor force changes. The national level also had to undertake a strong "selling job" to the locals on the business strategy plans.

A consultant to the unions concluded that the union representatives, even in the Swedish case where they were brought in at the beginning, had a difficult time affecting strategy (Hedberg 1979). He contends that the unions were usually modifying management's arguments and were torn by regional interests. However, the analytical skills of the white-collar workers were particularly useful. One of the union's achievements was calling attention to the impact of changes on local employment and getting the Ministry of Industry to grant special support for the mining towns. One assessment was that the union representatives on the personnel team, where they had expertise, managed to obtain a very good policy on workforce reductions, while the accounting/control group members, with little prior knowledge, had little effect. The union's collective bargaining experience appeared to have the greatest impact in the employment area. Bo Hedberg (1979), who was a member of the Working Life Center's team that consulted on the merger, concluded that the union's influence on the final plan was marginal, but that their greatest influence was in dealing with surplus workers and their participation on committees during the merger provided employees with the opportunity to learn a great deal about the industry and the new company; insights which would be useful to them later.

Allan Larsson (1987), took a different approach. He maintains that the unions were convinced that the merger was necessary and that the unions were able to exert considerable control in shaping the direction of the new organization, in changing its financial reconstruction, and in the introduction of new technology.

The restructuring of steel presented the first large opportunity to test codetermination, with Larsson participating in the three-person restructuring committee and the unions employing the Working Life Center as consultants. The use of the Working Life Center was an attempt to build up information and evaluation on the union side as a means of supplementing or replacing the information presented by management. A study by Jonas Leffler (1983) of some SSAB facilities went further and projected the union not just as a receiver of information but as a processor in setting up its own information system.

Schiller (1988), argues that the Employee Participation in Decision Making Act was not suitable for dealing with Swedish steel's closures and mergers. The unions were allowed to participate and were supplied with financial data, and their economic consultants presented alternatives, but the alternatives implemented were decidedly these provided by the companies based on economic reality. He concludes that political intervention played a larger role than codetermination in softening the impact of restructuring on the workforce.

Conclusions

Figure 4.1 presents a comparative summary of negotiations over downsizing in the cooperative committees. Negotiations in Belgium were a mix of adversarial and cooperative. The unions' ties to political parties dictated their reaction to restructuring plans proposed by the government. Unions that supported the party in power backed restructuring, while those out of power resisted. Militant local action raised the cost of restructuring by receiving government assurances that workers would not be dismissed. In Luxembourg, where the unions were cooperative, the unions were involved from the beginning in tripartite negotiations.

In Germany, Metall attained its objectives through both its political ties to the Social Democratic party and negotiations. When the conservatives assumed power, the union shifted its strategy to negotiations and took an adversarial position. It was able to resist restructuring plans or force their modification. The unions were assisted by their control over works councils and sympathetic company labor directors.

Japan, categorized as cooperative, consulted with the unions. The unions were aggressive in pursuing their annual wage demands and cooperative in restructuring. Their cooperation on employment was assured since steelworkers kept their jobs somewhere in the firm.

Sweden was the clearest confirmation of the typology. The unions were involved in shaping restructuring strategy from the outset. This involvement was consistent with the tripartite economic and labor policies that had fashioned the "Swedish Model." The unions lobbied Parliament for financial aid in return for their participation in strategy at each level. They insulated their members from the first stages of

Figure 4.1
Comparative Bargaining in Cooperative Countries

Countries	Bargaining structure	Environmental issues			Outcomes	
		Nature of relationship	Formal participation	Principal rules	Joint committees	Restructuring
Belgium	Centralized	Cooperative to adversarial	Negotiations	Plan for restructuring	Yes	Employment adjustments
Germany	Centralized	Adversarial	Negotiations	Pensions	No	Employment adjustments
Japan	Decentralized	Cooperative	Consultation	Transfer of workers	Yes	Employment adjustments
Luxembourg	Centralized	Cooperative	Partnership	Plan for restructuring	Yes	Employment adjustments
Sweden	Centralized	Cooperative	Partnership	Plan for restructuring	Yes	Shifting products, restructuring

110

Figure 4.2
Comparative Employee Participation

Countries	Statutory	Form of participation	Relative strength	Union control	Principal areas of participation in restructuring
Belgium	Yes	Works council	Weak	Yes	Work rules, information
Germany	Yes	Works council and boards	Strong	Yes	Work rules, employment adjustments, plant closings
Japan	No	Labor-management committees	Mixed	Yes	Information
Luxembourg	Yes	Works council	Strong	Yes	Company strategy, employment adjustments, plant closings
Sweden	Yes	Labor-management committees	Strong	Yes	Company strategy, employment adjustments

restructuring by receiving a commitment that their members would not be displaced.

Figure 4.2 presents a comparative summary of employee participation in downsizing. In those countries where works councils were legislated, employee representatives were often involved in the development of corporate strategy related to restructuring, as they were in Luxembourg and Sweden. But the direction of the effects of codetermination on restructuring are mixed. Restructuring was accomplished in Sweden without industrial warfare; however, in Belgium and Germany, plant closures and mergers were resisted. What is clear is that where there were works councils and codetermination, the workers were able to slow down the process of restructuring, often with the support of local government, so that the costs did not fall quickly on the workers. Instead the workers' representatives were able to obtain a commitment of no layoffs for some period or of income guarantees. In countries such as the United States, without employee representation at the strategic level, the costs of adjustment fell quickly on the workers and their communities.

The adjustment strategies used in the cooperative countries were: first, stopping new hiring and allowing normal attrition; second, work-sharing arrangements; third, transferring and retraining without layoffs; fourth, early retirements; and fifth, permanent layoffs with income supplements and relocation assistance. The centralized nature of collective bargaining in Belgium, Luxembourg, Germany, and Sweden increased the unions' political power and access to the decision-making process during restructuring. Unions in these countries were able to influence adjustment.

NOTES

1. Blanpain (1982) for a full review of Belgium labor law.

2. Abe (1989).

3. The *Wall Street Journal* (September 6, 1983). See Peterson (1986; 1987) for a discussion of collective bargaining in the first half of the 1980s.

5
Employment Adjustment

This chapter discusses the private and public programs aimed at providing steelworkers with income security. Public programs usually address the employment problems of more than one industry, and this chapter discusses only those public programs that had a large impact on steel. For example, a general discussion of the Canadian Industrial Adjustment Service is not included. Post-steel employment activities are also discussed. The focus of this chapter is on the outcomes section of the conceptual framework. The hypothesis for this chapter, based on the typology in figure 1.2, is that adversarial countries can be expected to leave the issue of employment security to employers and employee representatives, who negotiate narrowly defined benefits. In these countries, it is anticipated that companies and workers jointly share the costs of downsizing the workforce, and that an important form of workforce reduction would be negotiated early retirement. In cooperative countries, it is expected that the government would share in the design and cost of labor market programs, and the outcomes would be the result of wide-ranging, tripartite discussions. In these countries, it is anticipated that the government and firms jointly share the costs of downsizing, and the cooperative countries are likely to try to maintain employment through transfers and retraining.

Adversarial Systems

Canada

The unemployment experience in Canadian steel was different from the other countries in this study, and reductions in the workforce were much smaller. Employment in the steel industry has remained relatively stable, except for major layoffs during the recession of 1982-83 which were followed by rehiring. Between 1975 and 1985, steel jobs declined by 9 percent.

At Stelco, in the early 1980s, layoffs during downturns in demand were the typical pattern, along with a slow shrinkage of the workforce (see table 5.1 for employment at Stelco from 1975-1986). In November 1982, layoffs were announced for 4,000 workers out of 23,700. Depletion of inventories was also used as a coping mechanism for shortening delivery time. However, this approach required the rebuilding of inventories later on.

A study prepared for the Steelworkers Union indicates that, from 1978 to 1983, there was a shrinkage of 1,156 workers in steel from 97,270 to 86,114 or 11.5 percent (Allen 1985). The most pronounced decline was between 1980 and 1982. A study of the reemployment history of the 33,292 workers who left steel between 1978 and 1983 indicates that 21,093 (63 percent) were employed elsewhere, 2,568 (8 percent) had no job at the time of the study and received unemployment insurance benefits only, and 9,631 (29 percent) had left the labor force. However, following layoff, 54 percent had returned to their previous employer. This supports the idea that Canada followed a typical adversarial pattern of layoff followed by recall. Steel was broken down into iron and steel mills, pipe and tube mills and wire products in this report. Workers leaving jobs in the mills had a slightly higher propensity toward unemployment and withdrawal from the labor force. Well over half of those reemployed had found work outside of steel and experienced a decline in their income. This decline in income is similar to the experience reported in studies outside of steel (Hamermesh 1987; Jacobson 1978).

The same study looked at interindustry flows. Nearly 21,100 workers left steel between 1978 and 1983. Those who found jobs moved in almost equal numbers to the services, other manufacturing, and a category called construction, utilities, and primary industries. The highest proportion of workers who moved to other jobs in other manufacturing remained in metal-related industries.

An analysis of employment and age indicates that the tendency to leave the labor force was much more pronounced for older workers, 69.6 percent for those over 65. Of those who remained in the labor force, almost half of those who had been employed, 46 percent of those under 55, did not have jobs. As employment reductions took place in steel, the age distribution of those who remained has shifted upward. In 1978, 24 percent were 24 years of age or younger, but by 1983, there

Table 5.1
Stelco Hourly Employment, 1975-1986

Year	Hilton	Fasteners	Wire	East	West	LEW	Total
1975	10,522	631	1,239	941	541		13,874
1976	11,338	709	1,094	990	462		14,593
1977	11,634	770	1,134	1,026	473		15,037
1978	11,652	736	1,150	1,155	678		15,371
1979	12,296	784	1,195	1,201	633	276	16,388
1980	12,093	607	1,121	1,119	713	599	16,252
1981[a]	7,443	491	920	790	1,011	846	11,501
1982	10,136	519	927	943	634	893	14,052
1983	8,974	562	888	878	577	974	12,853
1984	8,747	666	893	704	742	977	12,729
1985	8,489	671	733	801	630	1,033	12,357
1986	8,207	697	683	597	592	1,049	11,825

SOURCE: Stelco.
a. Strike affected employment figures for 1981.

were only 11 percent in this category. Those over 45 had risen from 30 to 34 percent. This is a result of seniority clauses where younger workers with less seniority are the first to be laid off, and the greater mobility of younger workers who choose to move on when employment is threatened. Older workers were the focus of a report by the Canadian Steel Trade Conference (1985) since they were presumably the least reemployable. The report was not aimed at maintaining employment or resisting reductions, but rather at the encouragement of community-based assistance from federal unions, as well as counseling, industrial development monetary assistance, and early retirement.

The Canadian government did not undertake the same employment measures specifically geared to steel that were developed in Western European countries because Canadian steel has remained quite healthy. Employment security measures were left to negotiations between the employers and unions, with some government funding. Negotiations centered on early retirement benefits. These will be discussed in the United States section of this chapter, since the steelworkers in Canada are part of the same union as the American steelworkers. In May 1985, the steelworkers and the companies formed the Canadian Steel Trade Conference, which evolved from a factfinding group into an action-oriented organization with continuous services. In 1987, the name was changed to the Canadian Steel Trade and Employment Congress (CSTEC). Its activities include research on competitive materials and Canada's steel trade, lobbying for steel in multinational trade negotiations, and developing a program to deal with restructuring. The mission statement explicitly excludes collective bargaining from CSTEC's goals.

CSTEC's Employment and Adjustment Committee, made up of equal numbers of management and local union representatives, created an employment adjustment program called Helping Employees Adjust Together (HEAT). This is a job development and job creation program assisted by federal government funds. The program offers assessment, job search, training and relocation funding. To be eligible for this program the local union and the company have to be members of CSTEC (CSTEC 1988). Start-up monies, up to $5,000, are available to any worker management group that wants to review an employment adjustment situation and develop a project work plan. After the work plan is completed, the project is considered for funding. Among the possible project areas to be considered are counseling, skills training, relocation, upgrading, and training for new technology. Average employee costs are benchmarked at $5,000. The first projects were at Courtice Steel and Frankel Steel and involved career counseling, a workshop on job search techniques, employer contacts and assistance in forming a job club.

The consequences of workforce reductions in steel have been dealt with by a combination of collectively bargained and publicly supported programs. When Stelco shut down its open hearth, 2,000 workers were laid off in 1981. These workers were assisted by government agencies. Since 1981, Stelco has sought to use normal attrition, retirements, contracting out, and overtime.

Great Britain

Great Britain had the largest relative reduction of its steel workforce of any of the countries in this study, and these layoffs added to the high unemployment levels in the declining northern manufacturing areas. Employment security was a combination of private and public initiatives. Some of the private programs were begun by management, and others were the result of negotiations with the unions. British Steel Corporation's (BSC's) strategy was to close inefficient facilities and concentrate on production at sites with new technology. Some of the inefficient plants were in areas where BSC was the sole employer, and plant closures became a politically sensitive issue. The Trades Union Congress Steel Committee at first insisted upon employment guarantees, but management offered severance pay, retraining, early retirement benefits and job creation. The company also sought to create a climate for change through improved communications with employees and what it termed an active social policy.

The company and the unions negotiated an overall manning strategy, and in January 1976, the Joint Statement on Reductions in Employment Costs and Improvements in Labor Productivity was signed, identifying reduced manning levels as the key to improved performance. The unions agreed to this after receiving reinstatement of the Guaranteed Week Agreement which had been suspended in 1975. The Agreement specified that overmanning had to be reduced within two years. Low-cost plants would receive a preference, as would low premium shifts, and flexible worktime began. The level of negotiations where the subject of workforce reductions was settled gradually shifted from the Steel Committee to the local unions, and negotiations over specific crew sizes were concluded at the plant level. The company offered severance pay to those whose jobs were eliminated because of plant closings. In 1977, the local unions at the Clyde Iron Works, followed by the Hartlepool plant, concluded a plant agreement which provided them enhanced layoff payments for surrendering their jobs. The local unions adjusted the method of payment to favor the age structure of the workforce. Union members felt that since there appeared to be no prospect of keeping the plants open, it would be far better to leave with enhanced layoff payments.

The Steel Committee shifted its strategy from requesting alternative employment to obtaining the maximum benefits for the workforce. The company continued to communicate with the employees and twice balloted the entire workforce in order to test the support among them for its policies when these were challenged by the unions. In both cases, there was overwhelming support from the workforce for the survival plans explained and proposed by management.

In 1978, the Ebbw Vale steelworks and the entire East Moors site were closed, and that same year the Department of Industry issued a White Paper which endorsed management's view that the plants were overmanned and had to be closed. The company unilaterally introduced severance compensation, retirement, retraining, counseling, transfers and job creation. Laid-off workers received enhanced statutory layoff payments and earnings protection for up to 148 weeks. Under the Employment and Income Security Agreements negotiated between the company and the unions, the BSC supplemented statutory entitlements by ignoring the statutory limits of normal earnings which were above the maximum and supplemented the amount by 50 percent for the blue-collar workers and by 25 percent for those over 65 who were in other grades.

For those who were moved to other jobs, their new salaries were subsidized based on their age as follows: under 55, 20 weeks at 100 percent and 70 weeks at 90 percent, 55-59, 23 weeks at 100 percent and 96 weeks at 90 percent, 60 and over, 26 weeks at 100 percent and 122 weeks at 90 percent. There were also traveling and resettlement grants for those who had to move, and travel expenses for those who didn't move but had their travel costs increased. All of these were negotiated. Retraining benefits for up to 52 weeks were also possible and paid by the European Coal and Steel Community.[1]

The BSC received help for the initial cost of layoffs from the government. One author puts payments at an average of $12,000, going as high as $40,000 for the highly skilled, and Grieves (1982), who was managing director for personnel and social policy at BSC, places payment at the equivalent of 26 weeks of pay. Early retirement was offered for men who had reached the age of 55 and women who had reached the age of 50. Many of the employees who opted for this scheme took up a second career. It was reported that 65,500 employees took advantage of this between 1977 and 1984, of whom 47,600 were blue-collar and 17,900 were white-collar (Mixed Committee for the Harmonization of Working Conditions). Benefits for new careers included income protection and course fees and could last up to a year at 90 percent of previous earnings (Grieves 1985).

The BSC introduced counseling teams drawn from the workforce in the plants where layoffs took place. Interview areas were provided for counseling, and each employee was interviewed twice. The first interview concentrated on the financial aspects of layoff and provided the worker with provisional information on benefits. The second interview discussed future employment strategy. Further interviews were conducted if the individual needed additional assistance. In several plants, transfer to another plant was offered as an option for some job categories. The Redcar plant had to be manned when the Hartlepool works were closed in 1978, and some workers laid off at Glengarnock went to work at Hunterston. The possibility of transferring workers to new facilities, originally part of BSC's strategy of closing old plants and opening five new plants, was limited because of the large size of the layoffs and the smaller number of jobs in the new more automated facilities.

Job creation was the task of BSC Industry, established in 1975 as an independent subsidiary. The Board of BSC Industry included six union representatives, members of the Main Board and the chairman of BSC. Its task was to create new jobs in the areas of England, Scotland, and Wales affected by the steel plant closures and to supplement the financial aid made available from British government and EEC sources for investors willing to create jobs in those areas in which plant closures affected employment (Grieves 1985). The company committed about 50 million pounds to BSC Industry. It worked with the EEC, central government, and regional and local authorities to help local communities with job creation and regeneration. Incentives to develop new jobs included a cash grant from the government of up to 22 percent of the cost of buildings, plant and equipment, medium-term loans provided by the European Coal and Steel Community and the European Investment Bank. The government also provided teams for assisting in establishing new plants.

Local offices identified the areas most affected by the layoffs so that aid could be directed to the appropriate places. In each of these offices, a small team was established. The individual members of the team established contacts in the area to lend a hand to new firms or expanding ventures. Several strategies were developed to create new jobs in the regions affected by steel plant closures. One strategy was to obtain the assets of BSC-owned land and buildings and rent or lease out the land or buildings to firms outside the steel industry. Another strategy was to build new industrial units on land owned by BSC or to convert old works into small shops for new small businesses. The best known of these approaches was the Clyde Workshops Project in Glasgow, where 90 units were created for small firms. Rental began in January 1979, and within a year 60 firms employing 500 people had been accommodated; 48 of these were new businesses. This was an important success story because it was in an inner city area. Another strategy was to invest in firms that came up with a proposal. Investments were in the form of financing or renting plants and machines to the firm after they had received funds from governmental agencies and banks. BSC Industry also provided unsecured loans and assisted businesses in exploring other sources of finance, including equity participation from venture capitalists, government grants, government loans, European Coal and Steel Community loans, and commercial banking facilities. BSC Industry is credited with playing a major part in bringing the European headquarters of Mitel, the Canadian telecommunications company, to South Wales, where it planned to employ some 3,000 workers.

Another strategy was marketing. Advertising campaigns in the national, regional, and local newspapers sought to attract job creation projects. BSC Industry, together with the Department of Industry and the European Social Fund, offered a package of grants up to almost 80 percent of the cost incurred by firms conducting training programs at their own sites. BSC Industry is credited with handling 20,000 inquiries regarding new projects, helping 2,000 projects to operate, creating over 30,000 actual jobs in the areas affected by steel closures, and establishing the potential growth of a further 20,000 jobs (Grieves 1985). It reported that between April 1978 and November 1979, 207 projects had received support with job commitments of 7,050 and estimated employment of 2,400.

The BSC Industry Board presented a plan to the Main Board of the parent company in 1981 to provide funding for three more years. It was proposed that this money would be invested in assets for job creation. The prime objective of this effort was to make BSC Industry self-funding. In 1983, BSC Industry merged its local offices with local Enterprise Agencies to allow public and private sector resources together to support local teams, and nominated one of its senior executives to sit on the Board of Directors of each Enterprise Agency company. There were about 250 such agencies in Great Britain; 18 of them were in regions affected by BSC restructuring. Local Enterprise Agencies are independent community companies supported at times with as many as 40-50 organizations for the purpose of local economic development. In April 1984, BSC Industry became self-funding, its income derived from property rentals and interest on loans to companies creating jobs in closure areas. Grieves (1985) claims this increase was sufficient to cover total operating expenses.

An evaluation of BSC Industry by Young (1986) maintains that the only organization created as a result of the British steel crisis was BSC Industry, and that one of its problems was that attempts to find a private purchaser for any steelworks was always resisted by BSC's refusal to sell steel plants to the private sector for fear of new competition. Employment in new projects was also only a small fraction of total reductions (OECD 1980). BSC management maintains that it was a successful venture creating 90,000 job opportunities, 3,000 start-ups or expansions and 8 sites with 293 companies and 1,800 employees.

Public programs were provided by the British government and the EEC. These provided general and targeted employment security programs. Plant closings had to be registered with the Manpower Sources Commission. The Redundancy Payments Act of 1965 called for 30 day's advance notification to the government of individual layoffs and 90 days notice of layoffs of more than 100 employees. There were mandatory lump-sum payments to those affected. Revisions have strengthened the requirements for joint labor-management planning to avoid layoffs, but the basic structure has remained unchanged. The lump-sum payments for steelworkers exceeded the statutory requirements because there were "super payments" available from the government for the nationalized industries, particularly coal and steel. Discharged steelworkers at Port Talbot received an average payment of $15,000 in addition to their pension (OECD 1980). These "super payments" were well above the level of private company plans. In addition, super continuance plans could provide up to two year's salary or salary supplements for those reemployed in a lower paying job. Port Talbot workers received income supplements up to 90 percent of their former wage for the two years following their job loss. The maximum layoff payment was $18,000.

Government assistance was supplemented by EEC programs; there is, however, some question about how eagerly the British government sought EEC assistance. It was reported in January 1980 by Henk Vredeling, EEC Commissioner for Social Policy, that the government had not contacted the EEC for financial help in handling steel layoffs. A subsidy of $92 million (1980 $ US) had been turned down by the BSC. The government justified its refusal of the aid on the grounds that such subsidies might lead to work-sharing and inefficiency (Richardson and Duley 1986).

The reemployment experiences of discharged steelworkers were studied at three steelmaking facilities: Shotton (North Wales) and Consett (North East England), which were BSC facilities, and Llanelli (South Wales) which was a private firm (Iron and Steel Confederation 1980). For Shotton, the average age of the laid-off worker was 46. The average worker had been employed by the same firm for 18 years. Over 97 percent were male and 90 percent were manual workers. Twenty-two percent of those eligible for early retirement (470 out of 2,135) took it, while the rest preferred to look for new jobs. The largest percentage (32 percent) who choose retraining were under 30 years of age, and 82 percent of these were in the manual trades. At Consett, as at Shotton, most of the workforce (80 percent) lived within a three mile radius of the plant. Only 15 percent (135) took advantage of the early retirement option, and up to October 1983, 44.2 percent had undergone or were undergoing retraining. Seventy-four (25.5 percent) had found alternative employment, and 45.3 percent (1,550) were still registered as unemployed.

The authors of the study concluded that local plant management objected to the survey and that data on the unemployed and use of EEC funds were lacking (Iron and Steel Confederation 1980). They also reported that private-sector steelworkers received a much smaller total layoff package (when compared with the special payments available to the BSC plus an additional payment equal to 50 percent of the amount from the Statutory Redundancy Program). All of this was in addition to the ECSC Readaptation and Statutory Programs.

United States

The reduction in steel jobs in the United States was drastic. Fifty-one percent of the jobs were eliminated between 1970 and 1990. American steel companies rarely closed a plant abruptly. Rather, they retired individual facilities or mills in the plant after allowing them to wear down gradually over a number of years. Eventually, the entire plant could be closed, but most of the reductions in the past decade have came from partial plant closures (Barnett and Crandall 1986). For example, the Bethlehem plant in Lakawanna, New York had 11,200 employees in 1968. It reduced jobs in 1974, 1977, and 1981, and by 1984, only a small number of jobs remained (New York State Department of Labor 1988). Most of the closures were in integrated plants that produced bars and wire rods, two products that came to be dominated by mini-mills. Barnett and Crandall argued that integrated steel companies, rather than keeping obsolete steelworks open or building new coke ovens, blast furnaces, basic oxygen furnaces and continuous casters, appeared to be willing to rely on other producers to feed their raw steel requirements for a narrower and narrower line of finished steel products (Barnett and Crandall 1986).

Income security programs were negotiated between employers and the United Steelworkers. Davis and Montgomery (1986) argued that the steel income security network was designed to handle cyclical changes rather than the sharp restructuring that took place. There were no government programs that dealt specifically with excess steelworkers. The Trade Adjustment Act comes closest to meeting this criterion. Negotiated agreements were more extensive in the United States than in most of the cooperative countries where collectively bargaining programs supplemented government programs targeted at steel.

The guaranteed lifetime income protection programs were the principal source of income security for excess steelworkers. Kassalow (1984) cites a survey indicating that only workers under 41 years of age and with less than 20 years of service lacked lifetime income protection. All the others received, if social security benefits paid from the age of 62 are included in the overall calculation, some form of income security from the time their employment was terminated until the end of their life. The three programs that made up the guaranteed lifetime income protection was the rule-of-65 pension, the 70/80 pension, and the special pension window. An employee with 20 or more years of continuous service was eligible for a rule-of-65 retirement if age plus service added up to 65. An employee who had at least 15 years of continuous service could retire before 62 if he had reached 55 and age and service equaled 80 (rule-of-80). There was also a one-time special retirement program during the 1983-1986 contract. Medical insurance was also provided. United States Steel paid out over $550 million in pensions and medical benefits for retirees in 1985.

Relocation allowances ranged from $600 to $1,450 for married employees. Severance pay was calculated on the basis of years of service. Supplementary unemployment benefits, in addition to unemployment insurance (UI), were used for temporary loss of employment. The size of benefits and their length of time were calculated on the basis of previous earnings, length of service, the worker's family situation, the statutory benefits, and possibilities of reemployment. An employee with more than 20 years seniority could receive supplementary unemployment benefits for up to two years. These benefits were financed by the steel companies through contributions to a special fund.

Individualized bargaining in 1986 resulted in somewhat different programs among the large steel companies. The 1986 contract at National Steel Corporation established an Employment Security Plan. A guarantee was made that no employee would be laid off during the contract except under disastrous circumstances. Disastrous circumstances were defined as: permanent shutdown of a plant, rejection of the Plan in bankruptcy proceedings, or severe financial difficulties contingent upon agreement from the union. The Employment Security Plan also provided for flexible work assignments and reassignments across traditional job classifications within each plant. An employee who refused reassignment could be placed on a leave of absence without supplementary unemployment benefits. To administer the Employment Security Plan, each plant was required to establish a joint Employment Security Productivity Committee. Other related provisions provided limitations on contracting out and a $1.2 billion investment commitment from National.

Employment benefits created large pension fund obligations for the companies, which affected their operating decisions. A firm operates a plant as long as the revenues exceed the out-of-pocket costs, principally those for materials and labor. Pension plans in the steel industry turned part of the operating costs into a fixed cost, since laying off workers resulted in a substantial liability that was not affected by subsequent changes in output. It was argued that, since steel companies could avoid only part of the workers' wages through layoffs, they tended to keep more capacity operating than might otherwise be justified (Congressional Budget Office 1987). It was also argued that pension agreements reduced incentives to invest in labor-saving equipment because layoffs placed a burden on pension funds. Similarly, to the extent that a company had long-term contracts with materials suppliers requiring it to pay for inputs whether they are used or not, these inputs would also be considered fixed costs in making operating decisions. Employers' contributions to pension plans are largely based on previous experience, and the pension funds' resources may not cover obligations created when terminations exceed the historical rate. The amount of the deficiency becomes a liability on the firms' books. If a company is already in financial difficulty, the increase in liabilities can exceed its net worth and cause it to consider bankruptcy. When a company chooses bankruptcy under Chapter 11 of the Bankruptcy Code, the federal government's Pension Benefit Guaranty Corporation, generally by assignment or transfer, assures that workers covered by the plan receive their benefits. The Corporation was established under Title IV of the Employee Retirement Income Security Act of 1974. It is entitled to certain assets of the bankrupt firm. These benefits can be reduced, since the Pension Benefit Guaranty Corporation insures only a portion of the benefits. A firm may be relieved of the pension costs of laying off workers by declaring bankruptcy, while it continues to operate under Chapter 11. This policy would appear to subsidize the least efficient firms, since they are the ones most likely to go bankrupt; however, Wheeling-Pittsburgh, a large firm, and LTV, the second largest steel producer, both filed for bankruptcy under Chapter 11. By terminating its pension obligations, Wheeling-Pittsburgh reduced its labor costs over $3.00 an hour, which gave it a considerable edge in total production costs. In 1986, LTV had three times as many retirees as employees. LTV carries its pension obligations in its financial statements as liabilities, which means the company reports losses in some years, but if the Guaranty Corporation pays the pensions, these losses do not appear on the financial statements. The Steelworkers cited this approach and change in the accounting method of reporting pensions as liabilities, and pointed out that losses could have had an adverse impact on negotiated profit-sharing payments for 1988 (Bureau of National Affairs 1988). Pension Benefit Guaranty Corporation's efforts to restore LTV's responsibility for its pension plans, after LTV started to earn profits, were initially rejected by the courts. The Corporation had involuntarily terminated three pension plans covering 100,000 workers in January 1987 and tried to restore LTV's obligation in September 1987. They argued that LTV's economic position had improved, and the company and the union had negotiated liberal early retirement benefits. The Supreme Court upheld the agency's position in June 1990. Five of LTV's competitors had filed a brief alleging that LTV enjoyed a competitive edge of 20 cents per ton of steel by shifting its pension costs to the Pension Benefit Guaranty Corporation.

In March 1987, 81 percent of all Pension Benefit Guaranty Corporation claims were by steel companies' pension plans and amounted to approximately $535 million (USITC 1987). The 182 steel plans represented about 14 percent of the 1,345 plans terminated. Net claims or underfunding for the 182 steel plans amounted to $3.1 billion as opposed to $3.9 billion for all 1,345 plans. In 1987, Pension Benefit Guaranty Corporation was responsible for providing benefits to 151,900 workers in steel, 70,875 of whom were already retired. It was also estimated that the total underfunded pension for the five major steel companies (Bethlehem, Armco, National, USX, and Inland) was between $4 billion and $6 billion, which pointed up the possibility of more claims on the Pension Benefit Guaranty Corporation.

Layoffs in the United States, as in most of the other countries in this study, occurred in regions already burdened by high unemployment. The closing of the Youngstown Sheet and Tube Company was announced in September 1977 by the Lykes Corporation, which began a sequence of mill closings that permanently eliminated over 10,000 jobs in the Youngstown area in less than three years (Buss and Redburn 1983). Community groups in Youngstown, rather than the leadership of the steelworkers, took the lead in attempting to do something about the closing. Joint community and employee ownership through an employee stock option plan (ESOP) was explored by the Ecumenical Coalition, together with a government loan and a federal government guarantee that it would purchase steel from the Campbell Works for two years. The United Steelworkers were not yet committed to ESOPs and did not support the Coalition's efforts, which included its own locals, until 1977 (Fuechtmann 1989).

Government-funded labor market programs that assisted steelworkers were the Comprehensive Employment and Training Act, which was replaced by the Job Training Partnership Act (JTPA) in 1984. Title III of JTPA was used to fund several projects in 1989 targeted at steelworkers in Chicago, Allegheny County (PA) and Utah. The Trade Adjustment Assistance Program (TAA), provided for under the Trade Act of 1974, has been used more than any other government program to assist steelmakers (USDOL 1985). In April 1988, around 50,000 workers were receiving TAA assistance (ILO 1986). This program supplements unemployment benefits to workers who become unemployed as a result of imports. Under the Act, affected workers may receive retraining, job search, and relocation assistance, but the program emphasizes cash assistance.

It has been suggested that the costs to the federal government of the transition to a smaller steel industry could be minimized by forward planning (Barnett and Schorsch 1983). One option would be to focus federal policy on workers who had been displaced. The government could use its resources to set up a relocation and retraining program for such workers. Barnett and Schorsch have argued that reliance on the market is not an adequate response to steel industry unemployment, and that government help is required to retain relocated workers and attract new industry. If the federal government participated in a joint government-industry agreement to retire excess steel capacity, retraining funds could be targeted to those facilities closed under the agreement. They argue that job retraining could be emphasized in the program design, or made mandatory as a condition for unemployment insurance payments.

Proponents of retraining programs note that the retraining of workers increases the mobility of economic resources, promoting economic change and long-term economic growth. Critics, on the other hand, respond that job displacement occurs continually throughout the economy as a result of changes in tastes, economic conditions, trade, and a variety of other factors, and that a special retraining policy for steelworkers would be considered arbitrary and inequitable.

Information on the reemployment experiences of displaced steelworkers is available from studies by Buss and Redburn (1983), Jacobson (1978), the New York State Department of Labor (1988), and a report by the U.S. Department of Labor (1985). Buss and Redburn's study of Youngstown, Ohio present a micro view of what happened to 146 terminated workers. After one year, one-third were reemployed and one-fourth were eligible to, and opted to, retire. Some workers were offered temporary employment by Youngstown Sheet and Tube to close the plant. Small percentages of the laid-off workers sought retraining or jobs through relocation. They concluded that the Ohio Employment Service did not appear to have the manpower or resources to produce labor market information.

Most steel plants are located in declining communities. Jacobson (1978) found that steelworkers displaced in a local labor market with an unemployment rate 1.4 percent above the average suffered income losses over the first six years after displacement that were about 8 percent above the average. In a 1975 report, Jacobson estimated earnings losses of steelworkers displaced from jobs due to the removal of import restrictions. His assumptions are particularly worth restating, since they present an insight into the job tenure of steelworkers who are characterized as among the most highly paid and reluctant to leave the industry for any reason. Jacobson argued that attrition was not an adjustment strategy employers could follow in steel. Attrition was high among new employees and those near retirement; however, the majority of the steel workforce were in the middle tenure range, and there were few workers with low tenure. He concluded that steelworkers, if they follow the general experience of blue-collar workers, can be expected to suffer large financial losses even when displaced in a growing local economy.

The New York State Department of Labor (1988) study of the Bethlehem Lackawanna plant characterized the 3,000 discharged workers who were surveyed as an older, less educated, highly paid workforce with specialized skills that were not easily transferred to other employment. The respondents were white, male and over 45 years of age and averaged 29 years of service when laid off in 1983. Only half of those displaced ever worked again, although 90 percent expressed a desire to continue working. Their average duration of unemployment before finding work was 16 months. Those employed at the time of the study had averaged 1.6 jobs since layoff. Three years after the closing of the Lackawanna plant, only 38 percent of the displaced workers had found employment. Thirty-four percent of Bethlehem's former employees were still actively seeking work but unable to find it, while 27 percent had left the labor force for early retirement. Of those not currently working or retired, 76 percent never found a job. Those most successful at finding work had been laid off from the professional-managerial-technical occupational group, followed by electricians and welders.

The U.S. Department of Labor (1985) report cites a BLS survey which showed displaced workers in steel at almost 120,000. Steelworkers were compared to other displaced workers and were found to be disproportionately white, male, and married, with some high school education and skills, mainly as factory operatives, and with 10 years on the last job. They were unemployed 10-38 weeks after separation. Income support for this group came principally from UI and TAA compensation. Around 50,000 were receiving TAA benefits, including training, relocation allowances, and cash allowances. One-fourth of those who completed training were placed in positions related to their training, such as refrigeration, air conditioning, welding, computer technicians, truck drivers, mechanics, and electronics. At the time of the survey, about half of the displaced steelworkers had found employment. Reemployment was better for those in the 25-54 age group.

Cooperative Systems

Belgium and Luxembourg

Income security programs were developed at three levels through government programs, industry agreements, and company programs. In Belgium and the other European countries in this study, public and private programs were integrated and the public contributions reduced the employers' costs. The European countries, with the exception of Great Britain, preferred not to dismiss steelworkers, but to provide a number of alternatives such as early retirement, voluntary resignations, transfers, attrition, and reductions in the workweek. The Belgian government also provided training, a temporary reduction of the employers' social security payment for new employees, assistance to small and medium steel firms for hiring the unemployed, and loans to companies.

Normal retirement is 60 years of age for women and 65 for men, but early retirement plans began at 55 and were reduced to 53 and then 50 during 1984-1986. Early retirement payments amounted to between 70 and 85 percent of the worker's normal income before retirement and were composed of a combination of national UI and a company payment. UI was indexed to the cost-of-living. The formula for hourly workers required that the company contribute 50 percent of the difference between net income and unemployment insurance up to a ceiling of $1,221 a month (1985 $ US). For example, if the average salary was $757.83 a month, the retired worker would receive $437.88 from UI, and the company would pay $159.99 or one-half of the difference. Monthly early retirement income would be $597.84.

The metalworkers unions tried to spread the work through reductions in the workweek, and between 1981 and 1988, the workweek was cut to between 35 and 37 hours, with a continuation of the four-shift system. At Sidmar, the majority of those electing early retirement have been blue-collar workers, but white-collar workers, who perform less physically taxing jobs, do not choose early retirement (Stoop 1984). The government has also allowed nonsteel companies to start early retirement plans; however, these have been tied to new employment. Companies can offer early retirement, but only if they replace a retired worker. One estimate is that about 70 percent of the retired workers were replaced (Markey 1984). A recent law required 100 percent replacement if early retirement is granted.

Early retirement programs were usually negotiated with the unions. A national early retirement program for the steel sector, which ended in 1984, included men retiring at 58 and women at 53. Between the ages of 58-60, they received maximum unemployment insurance and $450, and an employer's contribution set at 1/2 of the difference between present retirement and full retirement.

During the 1970s, Cockerill began to explain to employees through its newsletter the need to reduce employment. In May 1977, it pointed out that tons produced per worker per year by its competitors were far greater than Cockerill's 206 tons. Usinor (Italy) produced 225 tons, Arbed (Luxembourg) 240, National Steel (US) 280, Sidmar (Belgium) 358, Thyssen (Germany) 375, and Nippon Steel (Japan) 524 (Cockerill 1977). At the end of May 1983, the redevelopment division of Cockerill-Sambre signed an agreement with a BSC firm, Job Creation, to examine possibilities for economic revitalization for 2,000 jobs in Charleroi where jobs had been reduced by 48 percent.

The largest reductions in jobs were at Athus and Cockerill (see table 5.2). Athus closed in September 1979, and 20,000 jobs were lost. The metalworkers unions obtained two concessions after a strike. One was the creation of an employment cell for 1,150 workers for three years— 1977-1980. This cell had the administrative responsibility for monthly payments to the workers and for ensuring their reemployment. The cell's members were entitled to their full previous salary during the first year, 90 percent of their salary in the second year, and 80 percent in the third year. The cell was jointly managed by the national government and the labor unions. At the end of the cell's term, in 1980, 550 workers were still without jobs (Capron 1986). The contract also provided for early retirement at age 55, with a supplement until normal retirement age. Workers not entitled to early retirement who were involved in short-term work or training received a supplementary award of $3.42 per day for two years.

The restructuring plan with the greatest impact on the Belgian workforce was the Gandois Plan of 1983. It called for the reduction of 7,900 workers by 1986 out of a total of 22,252 employed on January 1, 1983. Layoffs were to be avoided at Cockerill-Sambre, and reductions were

Table 5.2
Belgium Steel Employment, 1974-1983

Year	Cockerill-Sambre	Sidmar	Boel	Clabecq	Athus	Fabrifer	Divers	Total
1974	9,939,804	2,260,605	1,470,095	1,296,638	551,758	444,309	187,106	16,150,315
Percent of total	62	14	9	8	3	3	1	
1975	6,801,499	2,102,161	1,470,095	748,150	256,995	358,953	157,529	11,895,382
Percent of total	57	18	12	6	2	3	1	
1976	7,220,333	2,125,650	1,128,199	846,543	280,360	322,966	167,144	12,091,195
Percent of total	60	18	9	7	2	3	1	
1977	6,476,831	2,304,211	1,155,036	820,331	93,052	255,700	117,491	11,222,652
Percent of total	58	21	10	7	8	2	1	
1978	7,355,420	2,667,752	1,191,467	962,538		285,574	114,890	12,577,641
Percent of total	58	21	9	8		2	9	
1979	7,909,733	2,756,749	1,279,102	1,030,632		276,124	168,774	13,421,114
Percent of total	59	21	10	8		2	1	
1980	6,882,344	2,668,667	1,127,861	1,004,276		313,958	301,374	12,298,480
Percent of total	56	22	9	8		3	2	

1981	6,461,189	2,876,220	1,154,657	1,016,837	397,210	360,794	12,266 907
Percent of total	53	24	9	8	3	3	
1982	4,588,789	2,615,667	1,103,789		339,500	378,706	9,026,451
Percent of total	51	29	12		4	4	
1983	4,723,833	2,813,254	1,088,933		275,034	411,257	9,312,311
Percent of total	51	30	12		3	4	

SOURCE: Cockerill-Sambre, *Evolution Production Ocier Usines Belges*, April 4, 1984.
NOTE: Percents may not sum to 100 due to rounding.

to be met through early retirement, retraining and temporary quits. The plan was to be funded by the Belgian government, the EEC, and funds made available by wage levies on the remaining workforce.

Another aspect of the social contract in cooperative countries is extensive legislation regulating the termination of employment, particularly for salaried workers. This reduces the risk of immediate layoffs. The notification period is based on income and years of employment, and Belgian employees can appeal their termination to a labor court.

The Luxembourg General Statutory Law on Termination applies to steel. (See table 5.3.)

Between 1972 and 1983, Arbed cut its workforce in Luxembourg by 38 percent (see table 5.4). This was accomplished without dismissals by using an "anticrisis" model, which included establishment of an Iron and Steel Anticrisis Division, short-time work, early retirement, labor mobility, including training and retraining, establishment of a public works division called "extraordinary works of general utility," and establishment of a "new industries" department. The government supported this model by guaranteeing EEC loans to the steel industry of up to 10 billion francs and a subsidy of 30 percent of long-term loans for investment programs, and the Anticrisis Division was financed by an additional 10 percent subsidy.

The Anticrisis Division supervised a pool of up to 4,000 steelworkers whose jobs were eliminated (Wagner 1984). This pool was employed either on maintenance jobs at Arbed or loaned out to other companies at the same wage rate received by the workers at Arbed. This rate was subsidized by the government, which agreed to cover between 20 and 80 percent of the workers' Arbed wage and to grant a subsidy of an additional 5 to 6 percent of monthly wages with a partial exemption of employer taxes for up to two years. In January 1983, there were 3,700 workers in the Anticrisis Division, but by April 1984, the number was down to 1,000. Employees in this division were also removed from the cost accounting process of departments and not charged to the department.

Some of these employees were transferred to a government-run public works division, which had been terminated in 1976 and was reintroduced in 1980. By the end of that year, 650 workers had been transferred to it, and it also employed many of the Anticrisis Division members. Public works activities included maintenance of roads, plac-

Table 5.3
Luxembourg Blue-Collar and White-Collar
Notification Requirements and Severance Pay

Blue-collar			
Length of service	**Notice by worker**		**Notice by employer**
Less than 5 years	2 weeks		4 weeks
5 - 10 years	2 weeks		8 weeks
More than 10 years	2 weeks		12 weeks

Severance pay is:

Years of service		**Amount of pay**	
Less than 5 years		0	
5 - 10 years		1 month	
10 - 15 years		2 months	
More than 15 years		3 months	

White-collar			
Length of service	**Notice by worker**		**Notice by employer**
Less than 5 years	1 month		2 months
5 - 10 years	2 months		4 months
More than 10 years	3 months		5 months

Severance pay is:

Years of service		**Amount of pay**	
Less than 5 years		0	
5 + years		1 month	
10 years		2 months	
15 years		3 months	
20 years		6 months	
25 years		9 months	
30 years		12 months	

136

Table 5.4
Arbed Steel Employment, 1972-1983

Year	Employment[a]
1972	22,361
1973	23,004
1974	23,180
1975	21,986
1976	20,955
1977	18,928 (2,696)
1978	18,058 (1,913)
1979	17,737 (1,102)
1980	17,273 (2,129)
1981	16,613 (2,505)
1982	15,626[b] (2,877)
1983	14,016 (1,027)

SOURCE: Arbed, *Reports to The Annual General Meeting,* 1972-1982.

a. Numbers in parentheses are workers in Anticrisis Divisions in Belgium and Luxembourg steel and mines.
b. Includes mines.

ing of safety guides along roads, cleaning of rivers, and demolishing of old buildings. Schneider (1980) estimated that Arbed lost 20 percent on each worker. This removed them from Arbed's payroll for the time they were employed in public works. In 1984, the government funded a general works program that employed a quarter of the Anticrisis Division members, and job property rights were protected for the workers registered with the Division.

The workweek was also reduced from 40 to 38.16 hours, and overtime was discouraged. The government subsidized the pay of workers who had their hours reduced. Normal retirement had been age 65, while early retirement had been age 60 for blue-collar workers after 40 years of retirement contributions, age 60 for white-collar males after 15 years of contributions and age 55 for white-collar females after 15 years of contributions. This was changed in 1979 to compulsory early retirement for all workers age 57 or older. For the first, second, and third years, or until age 60, the worker receives 85 percent, 80 percent, and 75 percent of gross earnings. This is paid for by the unemployment fund, with a small contribution by the employer. After the third year, 70 percent is paid until age 65 for white-collar workers, and until age 60 for blue-collar workers. Then, the standard early retirement begins with contributions reduced by the missing contribution years. A June 1984 report estimated that nearly 4,000 steelworkers had received pre-retirement funds, and that 97 percent of all workers quit at 57 (Arbed 1984). A recipient of early retirement cannot return to the steel industry except under special circumstances and with approval by the Ministry of Social Security. Early retirement expenditures were met by the UI fund except where the worker was within three years of normal retirement. Under these circumstances, a contribution was also made by the European Coal and Steel Community fund. There was also vocational training in Luxembourg for new jobs, with two-thirds of the cost paid for by unemployment insurance funds. In 1977 and 1978, 848 workers were retrained.

The government added a mobility allowance to Arbed's severance pay to induce mobility. Mobility was facilitated by temporary pay of up to 95 percent of previous earnings for the first six months after moving, 90 percent for the next six months and 85 percent for the next six months. For those in steel, a 1979 law also provided vocational training financed by the state at two-thirds of the total cost, including 80 percent of the lower wages of the workers. The government agreed to contribute to training for new jobs, and to guarantee the EEC loans up to $341 million (1979 $ US) and 3 percent of the long-term loans.

A 1981 law established government-paid temporary reemployment subsidies for up to two years for those reassigned to lower paying jobs because they were in danger of being laid off. The subsidies were 100 percent of the former wages for the first six months, 95 percent of the former wages for the next six months, 90 percent of the former wages for the next six months, and 85 percent of the former wages for the next six months.

Before making a request for assistance from the government, Arbed had to inform and consult with the trade union organizations about the programmed reduction of employment, and employers had to report their vacancies to the National Employment Commission.

Germany

The steel industry in Germany used a large number of approaches in adjusting its labor force (Bain 1983). These can be understood only within the context of the politics and the nature of the employment relationship in Germany. The political background included the over-riding national demand for political stability since the Second World War, which could be seriously shaken by demonstrations over job terminations. The employment relationship more closely resembled the Japanese concept of permanent employment than the employment-at-will concept in adversarial countries. All employees, including managers, sign a contract with the company that can only be terminated by mutual agreement. An employee who is not satisfied with the company's terms for separation can and does go to the courts. A large number of generally accepted special conditions also give the employee job protection from discharge. These include length of employment, age, sex, and size of family. It is not clear whether the low mobility of the German worker is a cause or an effect of this employment relationship, but workers are extremely reluctant to change their homes, and the shortage and high cost of housing also retard mobility. This translates into a desire by the employers and employees to maintain the employment relationship. In steel, this long-term employment relationship was disrupted by the secular decline in demand for steel and a decline in the number of jobs by 47 percent between 1970 and 1990 (see table 1.2).

German steel firms adjusted their employment by a combination of a freeze on hiring, short workweeks, short-term layoffs, transfer from one plant to another, transfer from one job to another, retraining, transfer of work, early retirement, voluntary separation, and plant closings. Hiring freezes, short workweeks and short-term layoffs were used first. The company notified the works council and the employees that either a shorter workweek (kurtzarbeit) or a layoff of several days or weeks would be undertaken. The workers were eligible for unemployment compensation if the company had notified the state labor office and received its approval. In reality, the action is often taken first and notification given to the labor office later. The company pays unemployment compensation, later reimbursed by the state if the plan is approved, and the plans were usually approved. In addition to unemployment compensation at 68 percent of previous monthly earnings, the laid-off workers received payment from the company of about 22 percent, which brought their income up to about 90 percent of their previous monthly earnings.

Workers were also transferred, either permanently or for a limited time, to another plant; however, this approach was not used very often nor did it meet with a great deal of success because of the unwillingness of workers to be transferred. The most successful transfers were those where workers could keep their homes and merely alter their travel routes, such as in the Ruhr where firms had more than one facility. At Thyssen, employees who transferred to a distant site were offered company-owned housing. In transfers between jobs, the works councils played a key role in the wage decision. The first goal was to transfer the worker to another position at the same rate of pay. If this was not possible and the employee was dropped to a lower rated job, then the worker was given a "soft landing." This means that the employee's present salary was guaranteed for 12 to 18 months. After that, the salary was reduced slowly to the level of the new position by means of smaller pay increases.

The task of protecting job security was split between the works councils and the metalworkers. The works councils sought to preserve jobs while supporting modernization which they felt was necessary to keep the steel companies competitive and maintain employment. If jobs couldn't be preserved, then the works councils sought compensation. The metalworkers' approach was to negotiate protection against rationalization and to oppose plant closures and restructuring. Multiplant companies sought to develop uniform employment policies for all their plants; however, uniformity was not always possible because of the differences in opinions among the plant works councils as to how employment adjustments would take place. These differences could be attributed to personalities, the effects of the potential change on each plant, the availability of alternative employment, and the economic and social impact on the local community.

Several companies also sought to eliminate guest workers first; however, this was resisted by the works councils who were elected by all the employees. In 1982 guest workers made up 12.6 percent of the workforce at Thyssen and Bohler. In the same year Klockner negotiated early retirements instead of the dismissal of guest workers with the works councils, which had two Turkish workers (Mirow 1982).

Only a small amount of retraining took place, since management's position was that most workers were not capable of retraining. The companies preferred to fill new jobs with vocational program graduates who had received their training in company-sponsored programs. Works councils participate on the advisory board of these in-house programs.

Thyssen and Krupp adopted radical manpower reduction policies in the late 1970s, while Hoesch's policy was to close plants and reduce jobs. Arbed's Saarstahl reconstruction in 1978 required approximately $20 million from the federal and Saar state governments. Reconstruction in Saarstahl was accompanied by cutting wages between 10 and 30 percent and temporarily withholding payment of 50 percent of a month's wages. The workers were estimated to have contributed $80-$230 a month. The decline in jobs which began in 1978 was accelerated in 1983 when Arbed told the government that bankruptcy could be avoided only by placing 5,100 employees on early retirement. This included almost everyone over 50 years of age. These workers were offered 82 percent of their current earnings, and the unions were requested to take a wage freeze for several years. Management also volunteered to take a wage cut of 25 percent of their 1983-1985 earnings. After several weeks, the unions accepted the offer, since the loss of 5,100 jobs was deemed preferable to losing all 17,000 if the plant closed.

The works councils and the metalworkers favored early retirements as a method of preserving jobs and opening them up to younger employees. Early retirement programs were directed at workers who had not yet reached the normal retirement age of 65 for men and 60 for women. Under the state retirement system, men who have been covered for at least 35 years can retire at the age of 63. Early retirements were a voluntary program, either introduced by the company or negotiated as part of a social plan. Early retirement usually began at 59. For 12 months, from 59 to 60, the worker received unemployment compensation and a company payment which brought income close to the former wage rate. There was also an implicit understanding that these workers would not be offered new jobs by the labor exchange offices. At 60, former employees received retirement payments but at a somewhat lower amount than they would have received at the regular retirement age. The unions tended to regard the 59 to 60 payment as a subsidy for companies, since unemployment compensation was administered by the state labor offices out of a general fund contributed to by employers and employees; however, beginning in 1982, employers paid the entire amount of unemployment compensation from 59 to 60. This charge was pressed by the unions to avoid exhausting unemployment funds.

Voluntary separations were initiated by the company, negotiated with the works council, or were part of a social plan. Separations were accompanied by a buyout or cash settlement—"the golden handshake." The cash settlement was based on the worker's age and length of employment with the company. Election of a voluntary separation often had a time limit for the employee's acceptance, but voluntary separations that were part of a social plan could run for several years. When "the golden handshake" was first offered by companies, many younger workers took advantage of the opportunity to receive cash and then move on to other jobs. Older workers, however, were reluctant to leave, fearing they would not find new employment. To avoid the loss of their younger workers, companies began to reserve the right to refuse a request for separation. The role of works councils in separations depended on the size of the company and the size of the dismissal. In small companies with weak works councils, the companies have often dismissed workers without consulting the works councils; but in large firms, when dismissals exceeded 30 workers in a month, the works council has been consulted. Reductions in steel production and the installation of continuous casting in Thyssen resulted in reductions in the workforce. The principal forms of reductions at Thyssen since 1970 have been smaller hirings and pensions for those 59 and over. Where workers have been needed in the Hamborn facility, they have been transferred from facilities in Nederheium and Oberhausen within commuting distance. Voluntary separations have been very low.

A social plan, negotiated with the works council and approved by the labor exchange, was required by the Works Constitution Acts in the case of a plant closing. The first social plans in Germany began in 1957 in mining and in 1963 in steel. Between 1970 and 1974 in Saarbrucken, 92 percent of the social plans were negotiated because of total or partial closings. Bosch (1982) reported that personnel measures in social plans, in order of importance, were dismissal (87.8), reassignment to other plants (38.8), early retirement (17.4), retraining and transfer (17.1), and internal transfer (9.4). In one social plan in steel, dismissals for economic reasons had to be explained. Klockner managers claim that social plans were readily accepted by the steel unions. Plant closings were usually carried out over several years with slow reductions and employment adjustments which could include all of the methods mentioned above—from transfer to separation. The company began to close its Hutte-Haspe plant in 1967. The plant was closed slowly over a period of 15 years, during which time three social plans were negotiated—in 1967, 1978 and 1981—as the plant went from 7,000 employees in 1967 to 300 in the fall of 1982. The 1967 Hutte-Haspe social plan provided for early retirements and dismissals. Early retirement provisions for those who reached 59 included payments or provisions covering resettlement, a company pension, adjustment payments, anniversary bonuses, and special bonuses. Dismissal provisions included provisions for assistance, an employment anniversary bonus, and company housing.

The principal aspects of the early retirement provisions that most of the workforce used allowed early retirees to draw 12 months of unemployment compensation, after which they went on social security. These early retirees also received a monthly resettlement allowance for 12 months or until social security began. This allowance was not to exceed the present monthly net pay. If social security payments were delayed, the company would advance the social security money, which would be refunded when the retiree received payment. Disability payments were deducted from the resettlement allowance. If the recipient of an early pension lost unemployment benefits after six months, the resettlement allowance was increased. For purposes of the company pension, the years between early retirement and age 65 were counted as years of service. There was also an adjustment in social security paid by the company for those who retired early, because of lower payments into their benefit fund as follows:

Monthly gross earnings in German marks	Payment per month for missing years
Up to 1,000	10
1,001 - 1,200	12
Over 1,200	14

The adjustment payment was also due to widows and orphans, and an anniversary bonus was paid. Christmas bonuses were paid as if retired employees were active. After 1967, early retirees received Christmas bonuses as other retirees did. They also received their 1967 vacations. If the early retiree died before 65 and was not reemployed, relatives received payments conforming to plant orders in force at the time of death. Company housing also continued. The principal claims in case of dismissal at Hutte-Haspe included the same assistance as the coal-mining industry employees received under the European Coal and Steel Contract of July 12, 1966. Severance pay was equal to average contract net pay of the last six months net of deductions every month until age 65 or up to 12 months. The possibility of company retraining was examined with the labor exchange, and company assistance was granted. Anniversary bonuses were granted as due on the anniversary date if it fell:

within first 3 months	100%
within first 4-6 months	75%
within first 7-12 months	50%

Company housing continued for at least three years, and company loans for home building were renegotiated. The benefits were based on expectations of assistance from the government and the EEC. If these were not granted, the plan was to be renegotiated. Klockner would make advance payments in anticipation of these subsidies. An employee who received public support would reimburse the company.

The 1982 social plan, which ran until December 31, 1984, stated that the plant would shut down on December 31, 1984 or sooner. The principal clauses required that the company would make every effort to find work at other plants. A 1980 agreement from another facility was extended to this plant because of the manpower structure of this plant, which had 90 percent with more than 20 years of seniority, 20 percent handicapped, and 70 percent over 50 years of age. The principal difference between the 1967 and 1982 plans was that those born in 1926 or before, age 56 or older, were eligible for early retirement, while all others were to be dismissed with a payment of up to two years of net earnings.

Employees at Hutte-Haspe were encouraged to leave voluntarily through incentive payments of 50 percent of their final termination pay. Because of the plant closing, employees were not eligible for unemployment compensation, and the company made up the difference for up to 12 months from a "hardship fund." Workers transferred during the last two years into lower paying jobs in the company had their compensation tied to the previous rated job. Again, employees on early retirement who received maximum monthly benefits also got an additional payment. Those dismissed under the 1982 plan were eligible for retraining, transfer at the old rate, money expenses, and a resettlement allowance of up to $826 for those transferred to another division of the company (1982 $ US). Those dismissed with at least one-half year and less than five years of service received payments as follows: one-half year of service (15 percent), one year (20 percent), two years (25 percent), three years (40 percent), and four years (60 percent).

Increases for each additional year were 15 percent a year or a minimum of $721 (1982 $ US). A floor was established. Those without at least 10 years of service and 40 years of age received an additional 30 percent, those over 50, 70 percent. For special hardship cases, a fund was established, with the cooperation of the works council, to provide up to $206 (1982 $ US) a person. Dismissed employees received their vacation, and graduated anniversary money was provided for those who would have reached 25 and 40 years of service, respectively, during the next two years. Those who left before the formal notice period had their payments reduced. Management at Klockner reported that payments for early retirement turned out to be more than employees would have received without the social plan, since most workers would have left between ages 62 and 63 and would not have received the maximum retirement pay.

On October 1, 1984, the standard workweek of 40 hours was reduced to 38 hours without loss of wages. The German Confederation of Trade Unions reported that a survey by IG Metall had indicated that this reduction of hours of work had saved or created 7,000 jobs, or 3.3 percent of the total number of jobs. The Confederation of German Employers Associations pointed out, however, that employers did not consider this reduction in hours of work an appropriate measure for dealing with the problem of unemployment. The employers argued that the reduction of hours had no significant effect on employment and that a survey carried out among steelworkers before the introduction of the shorter workweek clearly showed that they would have preferred an earlier pension age to a shorter workweek.

Labor adjustment programs were a combination of federal and state programs, negotiated plans, and EEC assistance. The Employment Promotion Act of 1969 regulated training, placement, job creation, and unemployment benefits. In the case of workforce reductions, there were special allowances to facilitate short-time working arrangements, subsidies, and incentives to induce workers to accept early retirement. These incentives consisted of a combination of unemployment benefits and advance payment of old-age pensions under the general social security scheme. Legislation in force since May 1984 provided for the possibility of voluntary early retirement. Any firm that agreed to hire an unemployed person to replace a worker taking early retirement after age 58 received a government subsidy. This allowed the employer to pay early retirement benefits until the beneficiary qualified for a full old-age pension, normally by age 63. The purpose of the legislation was to reduce unemployment. After July 1, 1986 steelworkers who were laid off and at least 50 years old received from $1,843 (1986 $ US) to $2,469. Transition payments were also raised to narrow the difference between unemployment insurance and their former income.

The politics of plant closings were particularly important in Germany. State and local resistance to closings, when combined with pressures from the metalworkers, altered or delayed management's decision to close plants. The legal requirement of a negotiated and government-approved social plan allowed the political process to intervene. Political pressures and the requirement to negotiate layoffs and plant closings with the works council increased the costs of layoffs to employers and forced policies based on long-term human resource planning. Employers tried to neutralize these costs of adjusting the labor force by moving to fixed-term contracts, subcontracting, and leasing personnel. They also externalized the costs by transferring costs to the larger community, the social security system, or the EEC. For example, the cost of early retirement was borne for a long time by the unemployment insurance system.

Japan

Japanese steelmakers share the internal labor market characteristics of other large Japanese employers, that is, a labor force divided into regular employees and temporary employees. A permanent employee usually enters the company after graduation, receives continuous training, and remains an employee until retirement at age 55 or 65. When Nippon Steel Corporation reduced its workforce by 4 percent in 1975, the country was shocked. (Table 5.5 presents NSC steel employment.) Steel had symbolized Japan's industrial rebirth. Shortly before the reduction, in December 1974, the Employment Insurance Law had been introduced. It included an employment subsidy plan to help companies retain excess workers by reimbursing the company for 70-80 percent of wages to maintain employment. The unemployment insurance fund supported this. To be eligible, a firm had to have one-eighth of its workforce on layoff. Employers can alternate the employees it places on layoff and this is done in steel. Two other laws were passed in 1977 and 1978 which provided temporary measures for workers displaced from specified depressed industries, such as steel.

In spite of the cutback at NSC, steelmakers resisted discharging employees. No one was laid off by Kawasaki Steel in 1976, but overtime was reduced. In fact, the Mizushima plant added 550 workers to its 11,500 workforce. The average steelworker was 31 years of age, had nine years of employment, and was earning $10,000 a year. However, reducing overtime from 25 hours to 17 hours a month reduced wages by $27.00 per person.

Employment adjustment measures utilized by Japanese steel firms have included hiring freezes with normal attrition, long-term transfers to other firms, short-term transfers to other firms, voluntary severance, dismissal, in-sourcing of work previously subcontracted, subcontracting workers to other companies, permanent transfers, temporary relocation within the firm, and staggered or partial operations. Between 1971 and 1986, the number of temporary subcontracted workers in the five largest steel firms was reduced by 28,715 (17.7 percent) as the companies sought to maintain their permanent employees. The number of new hires had been reduced by 1978. The retirement age was also lowered. The government reported that retirement in steel, by the end of 1985, would result in 20 percent leaving at age 55, 17 percent at age 57 and 49 percent at age 60 years.

Transfers to related firms were possible as long as there was expansion, and in 1989 NSC reported that it had transferred 8,150 blue-collar and 5,253 white-collar workers to related companies. NSC planned to hire only one-tenth the usual number of staff, and for the first time since the 1960s, planned to hire no production workers; instead, it cut its workforce and increased wages. In an agreement between the top five companies and their unions, the compulsory retirement age was extended to 60 years. NSC announced in 1984 that the Kamaishi plant would close and that it planned to reduce employment by 2,400 at four mills over the next few years through attrition.

The policy of the steel firms in Japan has been to consult and cooperate with the local unions. Steelworkers have been used in new investment programs and transferred to other firms owned by the same company or to other industries. Nippon Kokan (NKK), when it operated its Fukuyama site at 41 percent capacity, sent more than 200 workers to Toyota, Isuzu and Fuji Heavy Industries. NKK currently loans about 10 percent of its workforce out of its Ohgishima facility to other NKK divisions. About 800 blue-collar and 100 white-collar workers are loaned for two or three years. The Ohgishima project of NKK, completed in 1979, was carefully planned to achieve the revitalization of the old Keihin steelworks. Even though a reduction of about 9,000 workers was needed in order to double the productivity of labor,

Table 5.5
Nippon Steel Employment, 1970-1989[a]

Year	Blue-Collar		White-Collar		Total		Total
	Steelworks	Other groups	Steelworks	Other groups	Blue-collar	White-collar	
1970							82,070
1971							84,641
1972							82,655
1973	55,618	2,349	15,306	7,127	57,967	22,433	80,400
1974	55,002	2,383	15,157	7,543	57,385	22,700	80,085
1975	54,694	2,600	15,215	7,901	57,294	23,116	80,410
1976	53,281	2,562	15,265	8,059	55,843	23,324	79,167
1977	51,868	2,453	15,220	8,243	43,321	23,463	77,784
1978	50,261	2,360	14,902	8,642	52,621	23,544	76,165
1979	48,437	2,264	14,259	8,768	50,701	23,027	73,728
1980	46,529	2,218	13,943	8,927	48,747	22,870	71,617
1981	44,964	2,074	13,830	9,058	47,038	22,888	69,926
1982	44,496	2,067	13,660	9,811	46,563	23,471	70,034
1983	43,666	2,565	13,155	10,643	46,231	23,798	70,029
1984	41,671	2,474	12,553	10,747	44,145	23,295	67,440
1985	40,988	2,480	12,420	11,272	43,468	23,692	67,160

1986	39,272	2,349	11,896	11,439	41,721	23,335	65,056
1987	38,731	2,292	11,206	11,964	41,123	23,170	64,293
1988	36,464	2,259	9,480	12,654	38,723	22,134	60,857
1989	34,724	2,099	8,791	12,463	36,823	21,254	58,077
1973-1989							
Absolute change	-20,894	-250	-6,615	-5,336	-21,144	-1,179	-23,993[b]
Percent change	-37.6	-10.6	-42.6	-74.9	-36.5	-5.3	-29.2[b]

SOURCE: NSC Labor Relations Department.

a. As of April of each year.

b. 1970-1989.

this was done without dismissals through retirement and voluntary shifting to the new Fukiyama works.

NSC and Kawasaki announced their first ever layoff of workers in 1986 in order to reduce labor costs. NSC would cut back its workforce by 30 percent, and Kawasaki accelerated its five-year plan to reduce its labor force by 24 percent or 4,500 blue-collar workers. NKK, Kobe Steel Ltd., and Sumitomo also expected to lay off workers early in 1987. The companies agreed with the unions that laid-off workers would continue to receive 80-90 percent of their wages.

The Ministry of International Trade and Industry (MITI), in 1987, requested a restructuring plan from each of the steel companies based upon its projections of reduced capacity. Table 5.6 presents the responses of five of the firms to MITI's request for a reduction of their workforce of 35 percent by 1990. NSC would cut 19,000 jobs from 65,000 and announced plans to shut down five furnaces over the next four years in an effort to lower its dependence on steel operations. First to be shut down would be Ktakyushu, Kamaishi, and Sakai, and later Hirohata and Muroran. At NSC, 9000 workers would be retired, 6,000 shifted to a new business, and the other 4,000 given unspecified arrangements. NKK reported a planned reduction of 29 percent from 28,000, 6,200 from steel operations and 1,200 from shipbuilding and the other heavy industrial divisions. Additionally, 600 researchers and office workers would be affected. This would be accomplished by attrition and transfers to new businesses. Sumitomo Metal Industries Ltd. reported that over a three-year period it would reduce the number of workers in its steel industry by 22 percent. Again, it would be accomplished by moving workers to its new companies and the workforce would be reduced from 20,400 to 15,900.

The 19,000-steelworker loss at NSC was based on the following projection:

Personnel at the end of 1986	46,000 (a)
Personnel at the end of 1990	27,000 (b)
Redundant personnel	19,000 (c) =(a)–(b)
Redundant personnel at end of 1986	4,000 (d)
Age limit, retirement, and national decrease	9,000 (e)
Personnel requiring personnel measures	14,000 (f) =(c)+(d)–(e)

SOURCE: NSC Labor Relations Department.

Table 5.6
Employment Reduction Plans for Five Japanese Companies

Company (date of announcement)	Change in employment (dates of change)	Number of employees	Method of reduction and numbers			
					Transfers to	
			Retirement and attrition	New affiliates	New ventures	
NSC (2/87)	46,000-27,000 (3/87-3/91)	19,000	9,000	4,000	6,000	
NKK (2/87)	19,400-13,200 (3/87-3/91)	8,000	2,500	4,500	1,000	
Kawasaki (2/27)	19,100-13,800 (3/87-3/89)	5,300	1,000	3,000	1,300	
Sumitomo No. 1 (12/86)	25,200-19,200	6,300	1,900	4,100 total		
No. 2 (3/88)	20,400-15,900	4,500	70%	30%	(3/88)	
Kobe (11/86)	12,000-9,500 (9/86-3/89)	6,000	2,000	4,000 total		

SOURCE: Industrial Bank of Japan, *Research Report No. 239*, 1988, No. 5.
NOTE: Employment includes blue-collar and white-collar.

The medium-term program to be used for the 14,000 redundant workers was temporarily stopping the extension of the age limit for retirement which had been extended from 55 to 60 since 1981; transferring workers to firms outside the company for three to six months; and layoffs and training, where all employees are subject to a combination of layoffs and training for two to three days a month. During this layoff, they are paid at 85 percent of their base wage (Abe 1989). In 1989, NSC reported that it had transferred 8,150 blue-collar workers and 5,253 white-collar workers to related companies.

The issue of excess workers occurred at NSC when it shut down some of its blast furnaces. Since these excess workers were unevenly distributed among the sites, transfers were planned by 1990 from four sites in the following manner:

Transferring site	Nagoya	Kimitsu	Oita	Total
Muroran	70	500	80	650
Kamaisi	50	200		250
Hirohata	200	150	150	500
Sakai	30	50	20	100
Total	350	900	250	1,500

SOURCE: NSC Labor Relations Department.

NSC pays a transportation allowance and assists workers in the sale and purchase of homes when it transfers blue-collar workers.

Sweden

Income security programs at Swedish Steel Corporation (SSAB) were heavily subsidized by the government and the unions. The first restructuring plan for SSAB, in 1977, forecast a decline in employment between 1978 and 1982 by about 4,000 employees as a result of a drop in production capacity of 25 percent, the closing of the blast furnace at Domnarvet, and the closing of several lime and sintering plants. The 1980 and 1983 plans estimated a smaller reduction in employment by 1987; however, actual employment for the steel group turned out to be lower than forecasts. Total job losses during the first stage of restructuring for all units of SSAB, including steel, were 2,990 blue-collar workers (23 percent) and 792 white-collar workers (15 percent) for a total reduction of 3,782 workers or 21 percent of the workforce. If 1979 is included and only the three carbon steel plants and the mines are included, steel-related employment was 15,960 in 1979 and 12,258 in 1981, and the total reduction was 3,702 or 23 percent of the 1979 employment base, which is quite close to the original forecast. Table 5.7 indicates a reduction in employment of 16.7 percent between 1980 and 1986 for the three steel facilities. SSAB, as most of the integrated steel producers in this study, diversified at the same time they were restructuring, and the purchase of non-steel-related companies raised total employment. Reductions were accomplished without discharges because the government, as the price of its financial assistance, required that this be carried out in a "socially acceptable" manner, that is, through early retirement or work creation for those not willing to accept early retirement. The 1983 company report stated that only 50 employees in the entire company had been terminated through the end of that year. The decline in employment impacted most heavily on the steel communities, which were dependent on the carbon steel mills for local employment, and on the mining areas, which had already been depressed by earlier mine closings. In 1978, employment in the plant in Oxelösund accounted for 26 percent of that town's total population (see table 4.2).

The government, through the Labor Market Board and its majority ownership in the company, played a major role in influencing the direction and manner in which employment reductions took place. SSAB was asked to extend the notification period to employees beyond the required 6 months with an additional 24 months for a total of 30 months. SSAB, replied that it didn't have the resources necessary to support excess personnel and forecast that about a third of the reconstruction loan would have to be used to finance employment reductions. The government responded with a special employment subsidy. Financial contribution also came from the Job Security Council, a joint effort of the Swedish Employers Organization and the Organization of Industrial Salaried Employees, in the financing of early retirement for salaried workers. The Job Security Council is funded by a one-half of 1 percent salary deduction from the pay check of all white-collar employees who are members of the salaried employees union. Swedish unions traditionally cover the unemployment benefits received by their members during the first year of unemployment.

Employment reduction measures were negotiated and agreed to by management, the unions and the government. The general labor market policy followed at SSAB included a hiring freeze with no new recruitment.[2] Reassignment vacancies were filled through internal mobility, and external recruitment was permitted only when inside recruits could not be retained or found. An informal labor market exchange was created for this purpose. A special organization was established for each department with surplus personnel. The employment costs for surplus personnel were borne originally by each division until a program could be worked out. Employees were offered three months' pay if they left voluntarily.

Table 5.7
SSAB Steel Group Employment, 1980-1986

	Facility			
Year	Borlange	Lulea	Oxelösund	Total
1980	4,795	4,429	4,534	12,758
1981	4,669	4,357	3,366	12,392
1982	4,194	3,882	2,805	10,881
1983	4,356	3,937	2,798	11,091
1984	4,388	3,968	2,857	11,213
1985	4,293	3,931	2,855	11,079
1986	4,189	3,763	2,680	10,632
1980-1986				
Absolute change	−606	−666	−854	−2,126
Percent change	−12.6	−15.0	−24.2	−16.7

SOURCE: SSAB, *Annual Reports*.

SSAB promoted new employment in communities where employment reductions took place. The Security Fund or wage earners fund was used by SSAB to start new businesses in the communities where the plants were located, and $19,763 was used successfully (1981 $ US). During 1984, a system of five separate employee shareholder funds was established within the framework of the National Pension Insurance Fund system. Profits were exempted from the funds if they totaled less than a half-million Kronen or 6 percent of the company's payroll. The Fund came from a 20 percent tax levied only on real earnings.[3]

The specific labor market measures agreed to between SSAB and the unions fixed employment levels. The 1982 plan forecast a larger reduction since it had a 1978 employment base rather than the smaller 1979 base of the 1980-1982 plan. Surplus personnel were to be given the opportunity to voluntarily transfer to new companies where they would be given work or retraining. These volunteers had priority rights to recall in their old departments. If voluntary transfers over four months were not sufficient, SSAB and the unions were to negotiate over the number and persons to be declared surplus. All this would take place over a two-year period. Early retirement programs, one for salaried workers and two for blue-collar workers, were later added to a 1980-1982 plan and a 1982-1983 plan.

Early retirement with a pension had been introduced in Sweden in 1972. To qualify for the general program, the individual had to be at least 60 years old, have received unemployment compensation during the maximum period of 90 weeks, and have little prospect of getting a new job with "reasonable qualifications." A firm that wished to reduce its workforce could offer its older employees a period of layoff with unemployment benefits for 90 weeks and thereafter a pension. These laid-off workers were seldom offered a job by the employment office while receiving unemployment compensation. The wage replacement ratio for the laid-off employees was equal to unemployment insurance during the first 90 weeks. Bjorklund and Helmlund (1987) conclude that under the government pension, the after-tax replacement ratio is between 70 and 85 percent for most workers. From then on until the age of retirement, the replacement ratio depends on the individual's pensions rights. The after-tax ratio is between 70 and 85 percent.

The SSAB early pension plan meant that persons reaching the ages of 58 to 64 during 1981 might be granted pension benefits. This was in accordance with the general company plan and usually meant receiving 70 percent of their pension-entitled salary. For salaried workers, it was between 2.0 and 2.5 times the basic pension index or 60 percent. At SSAB, three exceptions for blue-collar workers were: (1) early retirees received severance pay from age 58 and 3 months to age 60, when the government early retirement program took over; (2) from age

60 to 65 the company supplemented the difference between the government early retirement payment and 80 percent of the retiree's former wages; and (3) there was a payment by SSAB to the blue-collar union of $197 (1981 $ US) for early retirees to fund the unions social activities and the administration costs of these activities.

Early retirement was attractive to the company because it was subsidized by the government. The costs of early retirement included severance pay, commitments to a temporary supplement to the National Pension and Compensation pay, and the allowances to the blue-collar union for social activities and administration. SSAB paid approximately 70 percent of the early retiree's salary until age 65, and a supplement to the retiree's government pension after age 65. The supplement was agreed to because the government pension was based upon the total number of years a person worked, and early retirees would have had their pensions reduced. This supplement was equal to the difference in the reduction of the pension.

SSAB's financial obligation for early retirement was met by the company through payment to a private insurance company plan (Svenskt Personal-Pension Kassan) that covered its employees. The total cost of early retirement for SSAB workers between 1978 and 1984 was $24,229,256 (see table 5.8). However, SSAB's costs were offset for white-collar workers by approximately 30 percent from the Job Security Council; the joint Employers Confederation-Federation of Salaried Employees fund. For example, for the Lulea works, SSAB paid a total premium between 1981 and 1984 for early retirement of salaried workers of $8,966,156: the Job Security Council contribution was $2,648,089 or 30 percent of the total (1982 $ US).

The first early retirement program at SSAB for blue-collar workers was available from 1980 to 1981 for the mining division workers who were between ages 58 and 65. The company's obligations were similar to those for the white-collar workers, and the major difference was an additional $237 for each early blue-collar retiree to fund various social activities by the blue-collar federation. Blue-collar workers received 70 percent of the normal retirement benefit plus a supplement after 65 years of age. Early retirements in steel began in the middle of 1982 and ended at the beginning of 1983; they affected 738 workers in Lulea (251), Oxelösund (131), Borlange (311), and Division (45). There was

severance pay on the date of retirement by year and a relocation allowance from the Job Security Council.

Table 5.8
SSAB Early Retirement Costs, 1978-1984
(in $ US)

Year	Costs
1978	280,365
1979	1,719,082
1980	6,242,645
1981	11,107,518
1982	3,863,050
1983	182,732
1984	833,864
Total	24,229,256

SOURCE: SSAB, Group Staff Administration memorandum, April 4, 1985.

Once the companywide measures for dealing with employment dislocations were decided at the corporate level with the blue-collar and
white-collar labor federations, plant-level measures were negotiated at
each of the three sites between local management and the local unions.
The blue-collar layoff program for Oxelösund, dated September 1981,
required that all layoffs were to be completed by March 31, 1983
(Zachrisson 1986). There was special treatment for those with chil-
dren. The procedure for agreeing on who would be laid off began with
a discussion by managers and labor. If there was no agreement, the
issue would go to the central personnel group, then to negotiation by
the union and management at the company level or a final decision by
SSAB's main board. External recruitment was to occur only after internal recruitment. Employees received time off to work in joint labor-
management plant working groups. Union working groups would
decide who got the open position. The committee to decide on layoffs
would be composed of two employer representatives, one blue-collar
representative, and one white-collar representative. This committee
would try to find work, called temporary reserve work, inside or outside the company. Outside the company the placement offices in local

labor markets would be used. Employees could go to work outside the company for up to one month without losing their job security. In the new company they would receive a subsidy from SSAB's equal to their former salary; that is the new company's salary obligation was reduced by the amount of SSAB salary. Employees were obligated to take internal retraining during the normal workweek, and government grants were used wherever possible. The company paid for courses, books, and travel for study. Early retirement was at 60 or older. At Oxelösund the metalworkers were younger, about 38, and better able to be retrained while members of the white-collar unions were older, about 43, and considered not capable of retraining (Zachrisson 1986).

The entire process at Oxelösund was supervised by a project committee composed of personnel department representatives and trade union representatives of the Engineers, Foremen and Supervisors, and Industrial Salaried Employees. Reassignment and relocation were to be attempted first for surplus personnel by reassignment and relocation. Employment was guaranteed for two years, and hiring ceased. Advance notice of pending dismissals would be given to the Country Employment Board, the unions, and the employees. Identification of those to be reassigned would be based on persons whose tasks were discontinued, persons with the shortest time with the company and persons whose jobs were altered by more than 50 percent. Reassignment would be to vacant jobs, trainee posts, training programs directed towards specific trades and professions, a pension or other measures.

The Domnarvet Steel Works had developed a joint labor-management plan before the merger and restructuring (Gutchess 1985). In 1976, cutbacks at the works were planned for 650 blue-collar and 170 white-collar workers. The Domnarvet Council, with labor and management representatives, supported a main committee, which agreed that there would be no dismissals, and that plans for surplus workers had to be considered before organization and staffing plans were finalized. The measures, which were to be implemented over a two-year period, included a recruitment and hiring freeze and voluntary early retirement for all white-collar employees between 60 and 62 years and selected workers aged 55 to 59. Training was oriented towards specific jobs, and new jobs were developed. The plan Domnarvet used to reduce its white-collar workforce in 1982 after the reorganization into SSAB was quite similar to this earlier plan. The two-year plan for 225 workers included early retirement for those between ages 58 and 62, a freeze on hiring, internal advertising of job vacancies, training and retraining with pay, internal and external transfers with job placement assistance for those who were outside the firm, help in starting new businesses, and preference for reemployment of those trying outside work.

Table 5.9 presents the costs to SSAB of the labor market programs. The largest costs were in 1981 and 1982, when most of the restructuring took place. Divisions were altered, there were shifts in products, and no one was laid off. Activities engaged in by the surplus workers included painting and improving SSAB property, double-manning, dismantling facilities, retraining for steel and other work, formal education, day work, and extension courses. There were also costs for severance payments, salary supplements, and administration.

Conclusions

Large reductions in employment occurred in all the countries except Canada. If we compare declines in steel production with job losses, the first five countries are exactly paired. Starting with the largest declines they are Great Britain, the United States, Belgium and Luxembourg, and Germany. With regard to who bore the monetary costs of employment adjustments, the government bore a considerable share of the costs in both the adversarial and cooperative countries. There was some variation among countries within this broad conclusion, ranging from the least government help in Canada, the United States, and Japan, and the most in Sweden. The programs are similar in transition payments for early retirement, unemployment benefits, training assistance, and salary supplements. Steel companies were able to externalize adjustment costs and received direct payments, rather than loans, which subsidized their employment security programs. The government directly funded early retirement in Great Britain, training in Sweden, and public works in Luxembourg. In some countries, support was not given directly to steel but to a program such as the Pension Benefit Guaranty Corporation in the United States, or allowing UI to be used in the first year of early retirement in Germany, or the employment stability program in Japan.

160

Table 5.9
SSAB's Costs For Redundant Employees By Program, 1979-1983
(in $ US 000)

Program	Year					Total
	1979	1980	1981	1982	1983	
Painting & improving property	44.55		3,238.93	1,043.99	379.94	4,707.41
Double-manning	345.92	394.84	3,986.45	2,979.50	533.32	8,240.03
Dismantling facilities			1,026.98	1,518.82	172.82	2,717.96
Retraining - steel	927.67	458.91	882.81	1,043.68	430.67	3,743.74
Retraining - other	234.89	112.30	633.96	1,350.40	383.85	2,715.40
Education - below H.S.	14.00		131.73	336.80	80.60	563.13
Education H.S.	137.16	14.19	234.43	680.45	486.10	1,552.33
Education above H.S.	179.84	74.48	490.97	800.62	492.10	2,038.01
Third party, public works	209.70	235.25	178.93	298.28	100.95	1,023.11
Extension courses	.69		1.97	182.89	115.43	300.98
Severance payments and salary supplements			83.94	1,411.84	287.59	1,783.37
Administration	1,402.81	244.23	644.63	1,173.08	531.49	3,996.24
Total	3,497.24	1,534.18	1,135.70	12,819.69	3,994.86	33,381.67

SOURCE: SSAB, Group Staff Administration memorandum, April 4, 1985.

For the EEC countries, the government contribution was enhanced by EEC funds for unemployment allowances, retaining and resettlement. However, the origin of these funds was mixed, with half coming from a tax on the steel firms and half from each government.

Steelmaking is difficult work, and most steelworkers do want to retire when they reach their middle 60s; but they are not ready to lose their jobs in their 50s. New job creation for unemployed steelworkers has not been very successful. The service sector is not attracted to the old mill towns. Steelworkers were more likely to be unemployed or to have withdrawn from the labor force than the average unemployed worker. Those who found new employment were most likely to be employed outside of steel at lower pay.

NOTES

1. Local lump sum bonuses are not related to layoffs, but are rather a pay scheme tied to plant performance.

2. Larsson (1986), Nyquist (1986), Zachrisson (1986) and SSAB materials.

3. See Flanagan (1987) for a discussion of "wage earner funds."

6
Conclusions

The introductory chapter posed three questions related to steel adjustment. Chapters 2 through 5 then described and evaluated the process of restructuring in the eight countries, negotiations between labor and management, and the adjustment programs for the displaced workforce. This chapter summarizes the major findings through an examination of the three original questions.

1. Are there differences in the adjustment process between systems? Economic necessity required major restructuring in steel, including the shedding of a large portion of the workforce. The unions could not prevent these changes from occurring, however, what they did was to negotiate the pace of change and the size of the costs imposed on workers. In adversarial countries, firms had considerable discretion to proceed with restructuring, but they bore most of the costs. In the cooperative countries, the government restricted the freedom of employers to take unilateral action, but the government bore some of the costs of the adjustment programs.

Prior to the 1970s, there were stable cooperative relationships between management and unions in steel in all the countries studied here. Changes in this relationship in the 1970s and 1980s were not part of a drift in industrial relations strategy by management, but rather the result of competitive pressures. Unions found themselves increasingly pressured into accepting settlements they deemed unreasonable. The unions' strategies were fragmented either among unions in steel or between the national and the plant levels of the union. The Swedish white-collar and blue-collar unions had never coordinated their bargaining in the steel companies, and in Belgium the two principal unions—one Socialist-dominated and the other Catholic-dominated—had opposing political goals. Fragmentation meant the unions were either unable or unwilling to work out alternative strategies to plant closings. When confronted by management with the choice of either a reduction in the number of jobs or the closing of a plant, the steel unions in all countries first sought maintenance of the *status quo* or government protection. In the adversarial countries, the unions were excluded from the decisions to close plants. The Fairfield steelworkers refused to believe that USS would abandon a large plant. Only when USS reduced Fairfield employment and closed other plants did the employees abandon attempts to return to the *status quo*.

In the cooperative countries, unions were more likely to be included in the restructuring strategy. Sweden is the best example of union participation at the strategy level. In Sweden, the blue-collar and white-collar labor federations sought and gained participation in shaping the restructuring plan. The unions were able to do this because of both the tradition of tripartite decisionmaking and the support of legislation that required employee participation. The German metalworkers were also able to block restructuring until they were brought into the decision-making process, because codetermination legislation required their participation. However, even where the unions had some input into the strategy level, management was still able to unilaterally implement plans to cut the labor force, as in Cockerill-Sambre where 8,000 workers were shed without a joint decision. Discussions between the unions and employers were then limited to how to implement the layoffs, rather than whether or not there should be layoffs.

The steel unions were unable to mobilize the support of other unions or even to mobilize their own base. The labor movement was fractionalized in each country and there was little cooperation. The steelworkers unions had a history of receiving favorable treatment from the government in the form of financial assistance and special benefits, and other unions were reluctant to assist them.

There were strikes over restructuring in both the adversarial and cooperative countries. They were longer in the adversarial countries of Great Britain and the United States and considerably shorter in the cooperative countries of Belgium and Germany. In Great Britain, the government sought to break the unions and move to privatization. In the United States, USS sought economic advantage over its competitors. The short strikes were often a local initiative, as in Belgium and Germany. The national unions, in the case of these local strikes, were either excluded by their local membership or were reluctant to participate, since the short strikes didn't coincide with their national union policies. The principal targets of the unions' demands in cooperative countries were often national and local levels of government or the political parties, rather than steel company management.

Government had been friendly in Europe and North America during the 1950s, 1960s, and 1970s, when labor-oriented social democratic parties reduced labor-management conflict in steel. The steel unions had long-standing, well-developed ties to major political parties in many of the countries examined in this study: in the United States, the Democratic party; in Great Britain, the Labor party; in Belgium the Socialists; in Sweden, the Socialists; and in West Germany, the Social Democratic party. A number of deals were made. The steel unions were often compliant and cooperative in not striking and on some occasions agreeing to less than a maximum wage increase. In return, they received from the government subsidies, quotas and employment guarantees. This view has been advanced in the "corporatist" literature (Bruno and Sachs 1985; Crouch 1985; Calmfors and Driffill 1988). This arrangement broke down in the 1980s with restructuring and shifts to more conservative governments. Cooperation became either too financially expensive for the government or too politically expensive for the unions because of the potential loss of jobs of their members. At this juncture, the unions were faced with continuing to cooperate or face resistance from their members. On the other hand, failure to continue to cooperate meant the risk of losing political clout and the need to fashion a new political strategy. There was greater union activity in the cooperative countries, as in Belgium, or settlement through political exchange, as in Luxembourg and Sweden. Where access to political power was denied, as in Great Britain and the United States, there were long strikes.

Unions were most effective in steel where management needed their support to obtain government aid for financing restructuring or raising tariffs in Belgium, the United States, and Sweden. Special steel conferences of a joint or tripartite nature were established to deal with problems of restructuring and foreign competition. In the adversarial countries of Canada and the United States, these conferences were joint and private. In the cooperative countries of Belgium and Luxembourg, they were mostly tripartite and public. These steel conferences were in addition to the public manpower boards which had tripartite representation.

2. Which approach is more efficient from the point of view of labor and of society as whole?

The hierarchy of adjustment strategies from labor's viewpoint (that is, the more desirable the option the lower the costs imposed on workers and communities) are:

First, stop hiring and allow normal attrition to reduce employment.

Second, encourage workers to retire early.

Third, transfer and retrain without layoffs.

Fourth, establish work-sharing arrangements.

Fifth, lay off workers permanently, with income supplements and positive adjustment help.

Both adversarial and cooperative countries used options one and two; cooperative countries were much more likely to use options three and four, however. Layoffs were unacceptable in the cooperative countries because of the social contract, as in Japan, Luxembourg, and Sweden. In shedding jobs, consultation with the employees was likely to occur only in those countries that had a prior history of cooperation. Arbed's Anticrisis Division and its related policies represented a unique and successful approach to large-scale workforce reductions. This was possible because of the tripartite form of treating national economic matters and the consultative role of unions at the strategy level. Sweden's approach also has a great deal to commend it since steel restructured peacefully and quickly and its competitiveness was restored.

In adversarial countries early retirement benefits were offered to all older, senior workers who were laid off. In cooperative countries, early retirement benefits were offered to large groups of older senior workers as a mechanism for avoiding layoffs of all workers.

With regard to public efficiency, it could be argued that in adversarial countries employers could be expected to be free to restructure in a time-frame suitable to management, to quickly shut down excess capacity, restructure, and reap the benefits of gains in productivity. On the other hand, it could be argued that, in cooperative countries, the time frame could be altered to include the union's and government's goal of preserving jobs, which could mean keeping excess capacity open while workers were transferred or slowly retired. This could retard gains in productivity.

Two measures of public efficiency of the adversarial and cooperative systems, therefore, are how closely were adjustments in output and
jobs related to improvements in productivity, and how rapidly did each
system shed labor? Changes in productivity can be attributed to factors
other than labor, such as technology and managerial activities.
Broadly, however, we would expect productivity to improve when
labor is reduced. Table 6.1 presents steel labor productivity for the
eight countries over two decades, 1970-1990. Japan, a cooperative
country, had the largest absolute increase, while Great Britain, an
adversarial country which had the largest percentage decrease in production and employment attained the largest percentage increase in
labor productivity. Great Britain became much more competitive,
moving from last place to the middle of the eight countries when
ranked by productivity. The United States and Germany became relatively less competitive. A better view of what happened may be
achieved by dividing the two decade of restructuring into four continuous time periods and examining the three dimensions of output,
employment, and productivity together. Table 6.2 presents the percentage change in output (0), employment (E) and productivity (P) for each
of the four time periods and for 1970-1990.

The results of an examination of the relationship between output,
employment, and productivity are ambiguous. The largest increases in
productivity for both adversarial and cooperative countries were usually accompanied by increases in output coupled with declines in
employment, as expected; however, this was not true for Canada,
where employment increased, and for the United States, where output
decreased. There were no striking differences in the relationship
between output, employment, and productivity between the adversarial
and cooperative systems.

There is some difference between the adversarial and cooperative
systems when the timing of restructuring is examined. The period of
greatest job shedding for most countries was 1980-85. However, three
cooperative countries, Belgium/Luxembourg and Sweden, and one
adversarial country, Great Britain, began large reductions in their
workforce in 1975-80. This runs counter to expectations that adversarial countries would shed labor first.

The data do not support the expectation that adversarial systems are
more efficient than cooperative systems. The pace of adjustment did

Table 6.1
Steel Productivity in Eight Countries, 1970-1990[a]

Year	Adversarial			Cooperative			
	Canada	Great Britain	United States	Belgium and Luxembourg	Germany	Japan	Sweden
1970	240.5	127.8	218.5	218.8	192.2	273.0	137.5
1971	239.6	116.7	217.4	214.4	177.6	257.4	.
1972	242.1	126.3	245.8	241.1	201.7	293.7	n.a.
1973	300.2	136.6	265.3	250.6	223.0	380.2	n.a.
1974	265.7	114.2	256.6	262.2	238.7	377.6	120.1
1975	258.9	109.7	228.7	201.7	189.9	332.5	127.8
1976	273.0	124.3	251.7	209.4	202.1	355.9	122.3
1977	281.9	114.9	247.3	213.7	192.7	348.6	101.1
1978	292.7	126.1	270.4	273.5	216.9	364.9	117.6
1979	313.4	141.3	266.1	291.4	240.1	433.1	129.6
1980	312.3	105.4	244.7	291.1	240.0	453.9	120.2
1981	295.2	183.5	268.6	291.8	243.8	424.3	117.5
1982	291.9	197.0	219.7	262.4	226.1	421.9	131.7
1983	325.5	254.4	237.9	271.9	245.7	413.7	143.4
1984	356.6	267.9	268.7	329.7	293.1	460.9	169.8

1985	375.2	292.4	285.2	337.9	305.9	470.6	175.3
1986	371.0	292.1	296.8	347.6	298.7	454.6	180.4
1987	381.0	348.2	332.9	371.2	313.8	493.4	185.1
1988	417.5	388.5	362.1	436.4	361.5	593.9	196.2
1989	443.5	398.3	359.1	443.1	364.2	631.6	194.4
1990	431.2	390.3	367.5	463.1	351.0	660.6	192.4
1970-1990							
Absolute change	190.7	262.5	149.0	244.3	158.8	387.6	54.9
Percent change	79.2	205.4	68.1	111.6	82.6	141.9	39.9

SOURCE: OECD, 1970-1990 printouts, Paris, 1991.

a. Production in ingot equivalents per employee. Not all employees included in all countries and the data is not standardized for differences in the number of hours worked each year.

n.a.= Data not available.

Table 6.2
Percentage Change in Output, Employment, and Productivity in Eight Countries by Five-Year Periods

Adversarial

Period	Canada			Great Britain			United States		
	O	E	P	O	E	P	O	E	P
1970-75	16.34	8.42	7.65	-30.18	-17.67	-14.16	-11.31	-14.47	4.67
1975-80	22.03	3.30	20.63	-42.97	-38.78	-3.92	-4.12	-8.68	7.00
1980-85	-7.92	-21.05	20.14	39.80	-47.28	177.42	-21.08	-29.51	16.56
1985-90	-16.12	-23.09	14.93	13.63	-11.00	33.48	11.02	-10.71	28.86
1970-90	9.64	-32.00	79.29	-36.75	-76.35	205.40	-25.49	-50.84	68.19

Cooperative

Period	Belgium and Luxembourg			Germany			Japan			Sweden		
	O	E	P	O	E	P	O	E	P	O	E	P
1970-75	-10.29	-2.18	-7.82	-10.26	-6.65	-1.20	9.63	-6.03	21.79	2.00	11.71	-7.05
1975-80	4.50	-25.62	44.32	8.46	-11.04	26.38	8.88	-16.46	36.51	-24.42	-16.38	-5.95
1980-85	-13.64	-21.46	16.08	-7.62	-23.61	27.46	-5.49	-4.28	3.68	13.44	-18.28	45.84
1985-90	2.73	-21.82	37.05	-5.11	-15.78	14.74	4.80	-25.02	40.37	-7.48	-15.02	9.75
1970-90	-16.82	-55.33	111.65	-14.68	-46.57	82.62	18.23	-43.66	141.98	-19.09	-35.12	39.93

not occur sooner in the adversarial countries, and adversarial systems, with the exception of Great Britain, did not achieve larger percentage increases in productivity relative to their reductions in employment. The Canadian and U.S. peak periods of employment reductions yielded productivity increases of 20 percent and 17 percent, respectively, compared with Belgium/Luxembourg (44 percent), Germany (27 percent), Japan (40 percent), and Sweden (48 percent). Nor did they achieve these productivity increases sooner.

3. Who bore the costs of adjustment? In the adversarial countries of Canada and the United States, the companies bore the monetary costs of the adjustment through negotiated early retirement and severance pay; however, employees bore the personal cost of dismissal. Those who retired early still wanted to work, but they remained unemployed for long periods and only returned to work at lower pay. In cooperative countries, particularly Sweden, government bore the major monetary costs of adjustment as companies were able to externalize the costs through government aid in the form of partial or full ownership and income security assistance. In Japan, Luxembourg, and Sweden, personal costs were very low as companies retained their workers through transfers and retraining.

Both in the adversarial and cooperative countries, there was considerable assistance from government. Most governments did not have a specific steel policy, but there is no doubt that steel had a great deal of political influence and that governments viewed their role as preserving the steel industry through a trigger pricing mechanism in the United States, state loans in Germany, and planning guidance in Japan.

• • •

The market forces of new competition and new products that prompted the banking of furnaces and restructuring of the steel industry occurred outside of the collective bargaining process. Government action also prodded the earliest restructuring in both types of systems. Employment reductions were large and occurred in both systems whether they were a single-tier system of collective bargaining or a two-tier system of collective bargaining and employee participation. There was a difference between the two systems on the matter of cost to employees and the effects on a country's ability to compete. Cooperative countries were more likely than adversarial countries to retain employees, or to retrain and transfer them. This not only benefited the worker and his family but also the country, because it had retained a productive worker. However, the bottom line with regard to the steel industry of these eight countries and world class competitiveness has yet to be filled in.

References

Abe, Hisashi, General Manager, Labor Relations Division, Nippon Steel Corporation, interview and written response to questions, October 1989.

Adams, Roy J. 1988. "The 'Old Industrial Relations' and Corporate Competitiveness: A Canadian Case," *Employment Relations* 10 (2).

Ahlburg, Dennis S., Ann E. Carey, Bruce A. Lundgren, Sandra L. Barrett, and Lawrence D. Anderson. 1987. "Technological Change, Market Decline, and Industrial Relations in the U.S. Steel Industry." In *Workers, Managers, And Technological Change*, ed. Daniel B. Cornfield. New York: Plennum.

Algoma Steel Corporation, Atlas Steels Company, Dofasco Inc., Stelco Inc. 1983. *The Canadian Steel Industry and the Future of the Automotive Industry in Canada*, April.

Allen, Don. 1985. "Analysis of the Steel Industry Labour Market and the Adjustments Facing Its Work Force," *Canadian Steel Trade Conference*, Sault Ste. Marie, May 5-7.

Altmann, Norbert. 1984. "Company Performance Policies and the Role of the Works Council." In *Industrial Relations in Transition*, ed. Tokunaga Shigeyoshi and Joachim Bergmann. Tokyo: University of Tokyo Press.

American Iron and Steel Institute. 1978. "1977 Annual Statistical Report," Washington, DC.

Arbed. 1984. "Summary Report of West European Metal Employers Organization," 13th Plenary Meeting of W.E.M., Munich, June 7- 9.

Aylen, Jonathan. 1982. "Plant Size and Efficiency in the Steel Industry: An International Comparison," *National Economic Review* 100 (May): 65-76.

_____. 1983. "Technology Looks for New Directions," *Iron and Steel International* (February): 40-43.

Bain, Trevor. 1983. "German Codetermination and Employment Adjustments in the Steel and Auto Industries," *The Columbia Journal of World Business* (Summer): 40-47.

_____. 1987a. "The Impact of Industrial Relations on the Restructuring of Basic Steel Industry in Sweden." Proceedings of the Thirty-Ninth Annual Meeting of the Industrial Relations Research Association, Madison, pp. 201-208.

_____. 1987b. "Unions and Industrial Relations in Great Britain in the Past Ten Years," *Bulletin of Comparative Labour Relations* 16: 27-57.

Bamber, Greg J. 1984. "Relations Between British Steel and its Employees, Especially Managerial Employees," *Employee Relations* 6: 3-11.

Bamber, Greg J. and Russell D. Lansbury (Eds.) 1987. *International and Comparative Industrial Relations*, London: Allen and Unwin.

174

Banks, John and Kenneth Jones. 1977. *Worker Directors Speak.* Farnborough: Gower Press.

Barnett, Donald F. and Robert W. Crandall. 1986. *Up From the Ashes.* Washington DC: Brookings Institution.

Barnett, Donald F. and Louis Schorsch. 1983. Steel: *Upheaval in a Basic Industry.* Cambridge, MA: Ballinger.

Birmingham News, "Fairfield Shutdown Possible, USS Employees Told," July 19, 1979, A-1.

Birmingham News, "Roderick: Reagan Plan Would Boost U.S.S. Future Here," February 26, 1981, A-1.

Birmingham News, "If No Pipe Mill, Fairfield Works May Be Closed," April 2, 1981, A-1.

Birmingham News, "Fairfield Gets Pipe Plant With An If," April 2, 1981, A-1.

Birmingham News, "Pipemill Training Set, Other Jobs Still In Doubt," June 26, 1983, A-1.

Birmingham News, "Fairfield Mill Is `Rolls Royce' of Pipe Plants," November 25, 1983, C-4.

Birmingham News, "Wallace, U.S.S. Officials To Meet To Discuss Fairfield," December 13, 1983, A-1.

Bjorklund, Anders and Bertil Helmlund. 1987. "Worker Displacement in Sweden: Facts and Policies." Mimeograph prepared for the American Economics Association Meeting, December.

Blanpain, Roger. 1982. "Belgium." In *Encyclopedia for Labor Law and Industrial Relations,* ed. Roger Blanpain. The Netherlands: Kluwer.

_____. 1984. "Collective Bargaining in Industrialized Countries, Belgium." Mimeographed Draft of "Recent Trends in Collective Bargaining in Belgium," *International Labour Review* 123 (3) (May-June).

Block, Richard N. and Kenneth McLennan. 1985. "Economic Change and Industrial Relations in the United States' Manufacturing and Transportation Sectors Since 1973," *Industrial Relations and Economic Change.* Madison, WI: Industrial Relations Research Association.

Bluestone, Barry and Bennett Harrison. 1982. *The Deindustrialization of America: Plant Closings, Community Abandonment, and the Dismantling of Basic Industries.* New York: Basic Books.

Bosch, Gerhard, DGB, interview, October 1982.

Bradbury, John H. 1987. "Technological Change and the Restructuring of the North American Steel Industry." In *Technical Change and Industrial Policy,* ed. Keith Chapman and Graham Humphreys. Oxford: Blackwell.

Brannen, Peter. 1983. *Authority and Participation in Industry.* London: Batsford.

British Steel Corporation, Llanwern Works and the Trade Unions, "Memorandum of Understanding," May 20, 1980.

Bruno, Michael and Jeffrey D. Sachs. 1985. *Economics of Worldwide Stagflation.* Cambridge, MA: Harvard University Press.
Bryer, R. A., T.J. Brignall, and A.R. Maunders. 1982. *Accounting for British Steel: A Financial Analysis of the Failure of the British Steel Corporation 1967-80, and Who Was to Blame.* Farhborough: Gower Press.
Bureau of National Affairs (BNA). *Labor Relations Reporter,* March 14, 1983.
Bureau of National Affairs. *Employee Relations Weekly,* December 12, 1988.
Business Week, "U.S. Steel Is Changing A Lot More Than Its Moniker," July 21, 1986.
Buss, Terry F. and F. Stevens Redburn. 1983. *Shutdown at Youngstown: Public Policy for Mass Unemployment.* Albany, NY: State University of New York Press.
Calmfors, Lars and John Driffill. 1988. "Centralization of Wage Bargaining," *Economic Policy* 6: 13-62.
Canadian Steel Trade and Employment Congress (CSTEC). 1988. "Funding Principles," Toronto, May.
Canadian Steel Trade Conference. 1985. "Report of the Committee on Technological Change and Adjustment," Sault Ste. Marie, May 5-7.
Capron, Michel. 1986. "The State, the Regions and Industrial Redevelopment: The Challenge of the Belgian Steel Crisis." In *The Politics of Steel: Western Europe and the Steel Industry in the Crisis Years (1974-1984),* ed. Yves Meny and Vincent Wright, 692-790. Berlin: Walter de Gruyter, pp. 692-790.
Cockerill, S. A. "Le Nouveau Cockerill," May 1977.
Commission of the European Communities. 1981. "The European Automobile Industry," Supplement, Luxembourg, February.
_____. 1988. *Study of the European Communities' Re-Adaptation Aids in the Coal and Steel Industries,* by William Rees and R. Barry Thomas. Luxembourg: Office for Official Publications of the European Communities.
Committee on Tripartite Coordination, Luxembourg, May 21, 1981.
Commons, John R. 1934. *Institutional Economics: Its Place in the Political Economy.* New York: Macmillan.
Congressional Budget Office. 1987. "How Federal Policies Affect the Steel Industry," February.
Crandall, Robert W. 1981. *The United States Steel Industry in Recurrent Crisis: Policy Options in a Competitive World.* Washington, DC: Brookings Institution.
Crouch, Colin. 1985. "Conditions for Trade Union Wage Restraint." In *The Politics of Inflation and Economic Stagnation,* ed. Leon Lindberg and Charles Maier. Washington, DC: Brookings Institution.

176

Davis, Otto A. and Edward Montgomery. 1986. "Study of Income Security in Basic Steel Industry," BNA, *Daily Labor Report*, May 16.

Docherty, Charles. 1983. *Steel and Steel Workers: The Sons of Vulcan*. London: Heinemann Educational Books.

Dunlop, John T. 1958. *Industrial Relations Systems*. New York: Henry Holt.

Eason, I.V., Vice-Principal, Ashorne Hill Management College, correspondence, September 1990.

Economist, "West Germany's Steelmakers Feel Hot Breath On Their Necks," April 20, 1985, pp. 69-70.

Economist, "Europe Pays On," July 13, 1985, p. 72.

Economist, "Still Holding The Baby," March 29, 1986, pp. 23-24.

Economist, "The Strains on Europe's Steel Cartels," March 7, 1987, pp. 67-68.

Economist, "In The Furnace," January 23, 1988, p. 62.

Economist, "A Continental Future," October 29, 1988, p. 63.

Esser, Josef and Werner Vath. 1986. "Overcoming the Steel Crisis in the Federal Republic of Germany, 1975-1983." In *The Politics of Steel: Western Europe and the Steel Industry in the Crisis Years (1974-1984)*, ed. Yves Meny and Vincent Wright, 623-691. Berlin: Walter de Gruyter.

European Coal and Steel Community Treaty, 1951.

European Trade Union Institute. 1983. "The Trade Union Movement in Sweden," *Info 5*. Brussels, Belgium.

Financial Times, December 21, 1979.

Fischer, Ben. 1986. "Impact of Transition on Steel's Labor Relations," *Labor Law Journal* 37 (8) (August): 569-575.

————. 1990. "Labor Relations," *The Atlanta Constitution*, November 6.

Flanagan, Robert F. 1987. "Efficiency and Equality in Swedish Labor Markets." In *The Swedish Economy*, eds. Barry P. Bosworth and Alice M. Rivlin. Washington DC: Brookings Institution.

Freeman, Richard B. and James L. Medoff. 1984. *What Do Unions Do?* New York: Basic Books.

Fuechtmann, Thomas G. 1989. *Steeples and Stacks*. New York: Cambridge University Press.

Gerhart, Paul F. 1989. "The Ohio Steel Industry: Restructuring and Labor Relations in 1989," *Labor Law Journal* (August): 503-511.

Goldberg, Walter H. (Ed.) 1986. *Ailing Steel*. London: Gower.

Gospel, Howard F. 1983. "Trade Unions and the Legal Obligation to Bargain: An American, Swedish, and British Comparison," *British Journal of Industrial Relations* 23 (3) (November):343-357.

Graham, George. 1983. "Five Minutes to Midnight," *Metal Bulletin Monthly* (September).

Grieves, David. 1982. "Improved Productivity from the Restructuring of the Workforce: The Experience of the British Steel Corporation, 1977-1982." Paper for The 16th Annual Conference of International Iron and Steel Institute, Tokyo, October.

_____. 1985. *Restructuring in BSC: The Significance of Job Creation.* Great Britain, July.

Grunert, Thomas. 1986. "Decision-Making Processes in the Steel Crisis Policy of the EEC: Neocorporatist or Integrationist Tendencies?" *In The Politics of Steel: Western Europe and the Steel Industry in the Crisis Years (1974-1984),* ed. Yves Meny and Vincent Wright, 222-307. Berlin: Walter de Gruyter.

Gunderson, M. and N. M. Meltz. 1987. "Recent Developments in the Canadian Industrial Relations System," *Bulletin of Comparative Labour Relations* 16: 77-91.

Gutchess, Jocelyn F. 1985. *Employment Security in Action.* New York: Pergammon Press.

Hamermesh, Daniel S. 1989. "What Do We Know About Worker Displacement in the U.S.?" *Industrial Relations* 28 (1) (Winter): 51-59.

Hargreaves, Deborah. 1984. "Arbed Cuts Loss and Looks for Recovery," *Metal Bulletin,* May 1.

Hartley, Jean, John Kelly, and Nigel Nicholson. 1983. *Steel Strike: A Case Study in Industrial Relations.* London: Batsford.

Hedberg, Bo. 1979. "Worker Participation In Structural Change: Acting Out the Co-Determination at Work Act in the Swedish Steel Merger." Swedish Center for Work Life Working Paper, Isson 0348-3827, September.

Hoerr, John P. 1988. *And the Wolf Finally Came: The Decline of the American Steel Industry.* Pittsburgh, PA: University of Pittsburgh Press.

Houard, Leon-Ulric, Personnel Director, S.A. Cockerill, interview, May 1984.

International Iron and Steel Institute. *World Steel in Figures,* IISI, Brussels, Belgium, various years.

International Labor Office (ILO). 1986. "General Report," Geneva, Switzerland.

International Monetary Fund (IMF). 1990. *International Financial Statistics Yearbook,* Washington DC.

Iron and Steel Confederation. "ISTC/EEC Survey into the Effects of Redundancy Upon Ex-Steelworkers in the U.K.," *Iron and Steel Trades Confederation,* London (not dated).

Jacobson, Louis S. 1978. "Earnings Losses of Workers Displaced from Manufacturing Industries." In *The Impact of International Trade and Investment in Employment,* ed. William C. Dewald. Washington, DC: U.S. Department of Labor.

178

Kalwa, Richard W. 1985. "Collective Bargaining in Basic Steel, 1946-1987." Doctoral Dissertation, Cornell University.

Kassalow, Everett M. 1984. "Crisis in the World Steel Industry: Union-Management Responses in Four Countries." Proceedings of the Thirty-Seventh Annual Meeting of the Industrial Relations Research Association, Madison, WI.

Katzenstein, Peter J. 1985. *Small States in World Markets*. Ithaca: Cornell University Press.

Kochan, Thomas A. and Harry C. Katz. 1988. *Collective Bargaining and Industrial Relations*. Homewood, IL: Irwin.

Kochan, Thomas A., Harry C. Katz, and Robert McKersie. 1987. *The Transformation of American Industrial Relations*. New York: Basic Books.

Kochan, Thomas A., Robert McKersie, and Peter Cappelli. 1984. "Strategic Choice and Industrial Relations Theory," *Industrial Relations* 23 (1) (Winter):16-39.

Kozo, Kikuchi. 1984. "The Japanese Enterprise Union and Its Functions." In *Industrial Relations in Transition*, ed. Tokunaga Shigeyoshi and Joachim Bergmann. Tokyo: University of Tokyo Press.

Kunzman, Klaus R. 1986. "Structural Problems of an Old Industrial Area: The Case of the Ruhr District." In *Ailing Steel*, ed. Walter H. Goldberg, 409-433. London: Gower.

Larsson, Allan, correspondence, September 1, 1987.

Larsson, Allan, interview, May 1986.

Leffler, Jonas. 1983. *Fackliga Information System*. Stockholm: Swedish Center for Work Life.

Lehnek, Heinz, Personnel Director, Bohler, interview, November 1982.

Levine, Solomon B. 1981. "Labor in Japan." In *Business and Society in Japan: Fundamentals for Businessmen*, ed. Bradley Richardson and Taiyo Uedal. New York: Praeger.

Lipset, Seymour M. 1986. *Unions in Transition: Entering the Second Century*. San Francisco: Institute for Contemporary Studies.

Markey, Paul, Belgium Ministry of Economic Affairs, Interview, May 1984.

Masi, Anthony C. 1986. "Nuova Italsider-Taranto and the Steel Crisis: Problems, Innovations, and Prospects." In *The Politics of Steel: Western Europe and the Steel Industry in the Crisis Years (1974-1984)*, ed. Yves Meny and Vincent Wright, 476-501. Berlin: Walter De Gruyter.

Maunders, Allen R. 1987. *A Process of Struggle: The Campaign for Corby Steelmaking in 1979*. Hampshire, England: Gower.

McKersie, Robert and Werner Sengenberger. 1981. "National Practice in the Field of Large-scale Employment Dislocations." Report of the OECD, October.

Memorandum of Agreement Re Canada Works Consolidation Between Stelco, Inc. and Five Steelworkers Locals, April 27, 1984.

Meny, Yves, and Wright, Vincent (Eds.) 1986. *The Politics of Steel: Western Europe & the Steel Industry in the Crisis Years (1974-1984)*. Berlin: Walter de Gruyter.

Mirow, Eberhard, Personnel Director, Klockner, interview, October 1982.

Mixed Committee for the Harmonization of Working Conditions in the Iron and Steel Industry, *Questionnaire on Early Retirement Arrangements: Reply on Behalf of the British Steel Corporation*, not dated.

National Research Council. 1985. *The Competitive Status of the U.S. Steel Industry*. Prepared by the Steel Panel Committee on Technology and International Economic and Trade Issues. Washington, DC: National Academy Press.

New York State Department of Labor. 1988. "Bethlehem Steel Impact Study: Survey of Workers," Albany, NY, July.

Nyquist, Orvar, Executive Vice President of SSAB, interview, May 1986.

Organization for Economic Cooperation and Development (OECD). 1980. "Steel in the 80's." Document 8, *Job Creation by the British Steel Corporation in Major Steel Closure Areas*, Paris.

_____. 1982. "Developments in Steelmaking Capacity in Non-OECD Countries." Unpublished report of the working party of the steel committee, June.

_____. 1991. Telex.

Ovenden, Keith. 1978. *The Politics of Steel*. London: MacMillan.

Perlman, Selig. 1928. *A Theory of the Labor Movement*. New York: Macmillan.

Peterson, Peter G. 1990. "Japanese Mergers and Acquisitions in America," *Japan and the World Economy* 2: 91-106.

Peterson, Richard B. 1986. "Economic and Political Impacts on the Swedish Model of Industrial Relations." In *Industrial Relations in a Decade of Economic Change*, ed. H. Juris, et al. Madison, WI: Industrial Relations Research Association.

_____. 1987. "Swedish Collective Bargaining—A Changing Scene," *British Journal of Industrial Relations* 25 (1) (March).

Price, Robert and George Bain. 1983. "Union Growth in Britain: Retrospect and Prospect," *British Journal of Industrial Relations* 21 (March): 48.

Rich, E. B., interview, June 12, 1988.

Richardson, J. J. and G. F. Duley. 1986. "Steel Policy in the U.K.: The Politics of Industrial Decline." In *The Politics of Steel: Western Europe and the Steel Industry in the Crisis Years (1974-1984)*, ed. Yves Meny and Vincent Wright, 308-367. Berlin: Walter DeGruyter.

Schneider, J. P. 1980. "The Luxembourg Model of Anti-Crisis Management." Address presented to Management Research Groups, Nottingham University, March 27.

Schroter, Lutz. 1986. "'Steelworks Now?' The Conflicting Character of Modernisation: A Case Study of Hoesch in Dortmund." In *Ailing Steel,* ed. Walter H. Goldberg, 361-408. London: Gower.

Scheuerman, William. 1986. *The Steel Crisis: The Economics and Policies of a Declining Industry.* New York: Praeger.

Schiller, Bernt. 1988. "Workers' Participation—From Law to Development Agreement," *Swedish and American Approaches to Contemporary Issues: Labor/Management Seminar Series,* Stockholm: Swedish Institute, May.

Sherer, Peter D. 1991. *Industrial Restructuring and Industrial Relations in Three United States Firms.* Geneva: International Labor Office.

SSAB Annual Report, 1978.

SSAB Annual Report, 1982.

SSAB Annual Report, 1986.

SSAB Memo, not dated.

Stoop, Martin De, Personnel Department, Sidmar, interview, May 1984.

Streeck, Wolfgang. 1984. "Guaranteed Employment, Flexible Manpower Use, and Cooperative Manpower Management: A Trend Towards Convergence?" In *Industrial Relations in Transition,* ed. Tokunaga Shigeyoshi and Joachim Bergmann. Tokyo: University of Tokyo Press.

Thelen, Kathleen. 1987. "Codetermination and Industrial Adjustment in the German Steel Industry: A Comparative Interpretation," *California Management Review,* 29 (3) (Spring): 134-148.

Thimm, Alfred L. 1980. *The False Promise of Codetermination.* Lexington Massachusetts: D. C. Heath.

_____. 1987. "Codetermination and Industrial Policy: The Special Case of the German Steel Industry," *California Management Review,* 29, 3 (Spring): 115-133.

Torrence, William O. 1989. "Labor and Management Cooperation in Restructuring Steel Firms," *Labor Law Journal* 40 (8) (August): 496-503.

Tsoukalis, Loukas and Robert Strauss. 1986. "Community Policies on Steel, 1974-1982: A Case of Collective Management." In *The Politics of Steel: Western Europe and the Steel Industry in the Crisis Years (1974-1984),* ed. Yves Meny and Vincent Wright, 186- 221. Berlin: Walter de Gruyter.

Ulman, Lloyd. 1987. "Who Wanted Collective Bargaining in the First Place." Proceedings of the Thirty-Ninth Annual Meeting of the Industrial Relations Research Association, Madison, WI.

United States Department of Labor (USDOL). 1985. "Causes and Remedies for Displacement of Steel Workers: An Analysis of the Characteristics of

Displaced Steel Workers and of Programs Designed to Assist Their Readjustment," April.
United States International Trade Commission (USITC). 1987. "Annual Survey Concerning Competitive Conditions in the Steel Industry and Industry Efforts to Adjust and Modernize," Washington, DC, September.
Upham, M. 1980. "British Steel: Retrospect and Prospect," *Industrial Relations Journal* 8: 5-21.
Vaizey, John. 1974. *The History of British Steel.* London: Weidenfeld and Nicolson.
Van Den Hof, Karel, Personnel Manager, Sidmar, interview, May 1984.
Wagner, Marcel, Personnel Manager, Arbed, interview, May 1984.
Wall Street Journal, "In Sweden, Industry-by-Industry Talks May Replace National Labor Negotiations," September 6, 1983.
Wall Street Journal, "Two Steel Firms In Germany Plan To Merge In 1985," October 25, 1984, p. 37.
Wall Street Journal, October 6, 1987, p. 31.
Wall Street Journal, "Three Steel Makers In Germany Plan Joint Operations," November 27, 1987, p. 8.
Wall Street Journal, "EC Commission Reduces Protection For Steelmakers," January 7, 1988, p. 16.
Wall Street Journal, January 28, 1988, p. 20.
Wall Street Journal, "Privatization on Track With British Steel, Success Expected In Spite of Industries' Uncertainties," November 16, 1988, p. A-14.
Webb, Sidney and Beatrice. 1897. *Industrial Democracy.* London: Longmans.
Williams, D. C., General Manager, Personnel and Industrial Relations, Stelco Inc., interview, August 1988.
Windmuller, John P. and Alan Gladstone (Eds.) 1984. *Employers Associations and Industrial Relations: A Comparative Study.* Oxford: Clarendon Press.
Yamawaki, Hideki. 1988. "Chapter II- The Steel Industry." In *Industrial Policy of Japan,* eds. R. Komiya, M. Okuno and K. Suzumnna. San Diego: Academic Press.
Young, S. 1986. "The Implementation of Britain's National Steel Strategy at the Local Level." In *The Politics of Steel: Western Europe and the Steel Industry in the Crisis Years (1974-1984),* ed. Yves Meny and Vincent Wright, 368-415. Berlin: Walter de Gruyter.
Zachrisson, Per. SSAB, interview, May 1986.

INDEX

Abe, Hisashi, 100, 111n2, 152
Adams, Roy J., 55, 56
Adjustment process
  costs of, 171
  effectiveness of strategies for, 166
  nature and determinants of
    strategies for, 3, 8-9, 13-53
Adversarial industrial relations systems
  changes in productivity in, 167-71
  costs of adjustment in, 171
  countries with, 8, 10-11
  employment adjustment in, 113-29
  restructuring in, 15-24, 49-52
  See also Canada; Great Britain;
  United States
Ahlburg, Dennis S., 70
Algoma Steel Corporation, 16
Allen, Don, 114
Altmann, Norbert, 95
Anticrisis model. *See* Iron and Steel
  Anticrisis Division, Luxembourg
Arbed, 136t, 137
Aylen, Jonathan, 2, 13

Bain, George, 58
Bain, Trevor, 58, 103, 138
Bamber, Greg J., 8, 58, 59
Banks, John, 64, 84n3
Barnett, Donald F., 2, 15, 123, 127
Belgium
  collective bargaining in, 85-90, 108
  employment adjustment in, 130-34
  restructuring of steel industry in, 24-
    28
Bjorklund, Anders, 155
Blanpain, Roger, 86, 111n1
Block, Richard N., 70
Bluestone, Barry, 8
BNA (Bureau of National Affairs), 70,
  126
Bosch, Gerhard, 142
Bradbury, John H., 15

Brannen, Peter, 62, 63, 84n3
Brignall, T. J., 17, 58-59
British Steel Corporation (BSC), 17-19
  BSC Industry, 119-21
  contributions to BSC Industry by,
    120
  government subsidies for, 119
  labor-management relations of, 58-
    59
Bruno, Michael, 165
Bryer, R. A., 17, 58-59
BSC. *See* British Steel Corporation
  (BSC)
BSC Industry, 119-21
Business Week, 70
Buss, Terry F., 15, 127, 128

Calmfors, Lars, 165
Canada
  collective bargaining in, 55-57
  employment adjustment in, 113-17
  restructuring of steel industry in, 15-
    16
Canadian Steel Trade and Employment
  Congress (CSTEC), 116
Canadian Steel Trade Conference
  (1985), 116
Capacity reduction
  EEC role in, 39-49
  Japan, 32-33
  Sweden, 37
Cappelli, Peter, 3
Capron, Michel, 52n3, 87, 131
Christian Trade Union Confederation,
  Belgium, 86, 88
Claes Plan, Belgium, 87
Clyde Workshops Project, Scotland,
  120
Coal and Steel Treaty (1951), 45
Cockerill, S. A., 131
Codetermination, Germany, 91, 94, 97-
  99, 111, 164

183

Kalwa, Richard W., 68, 69, 70
Kassalow, Everett M., 3, 68, 124
Katz, Harry C., 3, 67
Katzenstein, Peter J., 8
Kelly, John, 61
Kochan, Thomas A., 3, 67
Kozo, Kikuchi, 100

Labor directors
    in Europe, 85
    in Germany, 90-91
Labor force. *See* Workforce reduction
Labor Market Board, Sweden, 153
Labor market exchange, Sweden, 154
Labor mobility, Canada, 115-16
Labor movement, 164
Labor productivity
    British steel industry, 19
    Germany, 99
    related to restructuring, 167-70
    United States, 23
Lansbury, Russell D., 8
Larsson, Allan, 38, 103-4, 105, 107,
    161n2
Layoffs
    avoidance of, 40
    alternatives to, 166
    effect of integrated steel industry, 15
    Belgium-Luxembourg, 26-27, 131
    Canada, 114
    Germany, 96-97, 139
    Great Britain, 59-60, 117-20, 121-22
    Japan, 150, 152
    Sweden, 155, 157
    United States, 74, 127-29
Leffler, Jonas, 107
Lehnek, Heinz, 97
Levine, Solomon B., 99
Lipset, Seymour M., 8
Luxembourg
    collective bargaining in, 89-90, 108
    employment adjustment in, 134-38
    restructuring of steel industry in, 24-
    28

MacGregor, Ian, 18
McKersie, Robert, 3, 8
McLennan, Kenneth, 70
Management council, Japan, 100
Market forces, 1
Markey, Paul, 131
Masi, Anthony C., 33
Maunders, A. R., 17, 58-59, 60
Medical insurance, United States, 124
Medoff, James L., 8
Meltz, N. M., 55
Meny, Yves, 2
Mergers
    Germany, 29-31
    Sweden, 36, 52, 103, 105
    United States, 20-21, 52
Metal Workers Union, Belgium, 25, 88
Meyer, Jerry, 81, 84
Ministry of International Trade and
    Industry (MITI), Japan, 33, 52, 150
Mirow, Eberhard, 140
Modernization
    Germany, 30
    United States, 71-74, 76-78, 81
Montgomery, Edward, 123

Nationalization
    Belgium: of Cockerill-Sambre, 24-
    25
    Great Britain, 17, 62, 63
    Sweden, 35, 36
National Labor Council, Belgium, 86
National Pension Insurance Fund,
    Sweden, 154-55
National Research Council, 52n2
New York State Department of Labor,
    123, 128, 129
Nicholson, Nigel, 61
Nippon Kokan (NKK), 21, 32-34
Nippon Steel Corporation (NSC), 32-
    35, 100-101
Nyquist, Orvar, 104, 161n2

Sidmar, 24, 25
Social contract
   in cooperative countries, 134
   effect of 1970s, 1
   recognition of, 3
Social Fund, 45, 46t, 47, 49, 121
Socialist-Christian Confederation,
   Luxembourg, 89
Socialist Confederation, Luxembourg,
   89
Social policy
   of European Economic Community,
      45-49, 50t
   German cooperative worker-
      management, 96-97
   in Germany, 31, 96-97, 141-44
   Great Britain: of British Steel
      Corporation, 18
Social security benefits
   in Germany, 142-43, 145
   United States, 124
SSAB. *See* Swedish Steel Corporation
   (SSAB)
SSAB Annual Reports, 35, 37, 38
SSAB Memo, 36
Steel-Town Group, Sweden, 35
Steel Tripartite Commission, 27-28
Stelco, 15-16, 56-57
   employment experience of, 114
   union-management relations, 55-57
Stoop, Martin de, 130
Streeck, Wolfgang, 94
Strikes
   Belgium-Luxembourg, 24-25, 87-88
   Canada: in 1981, 56-57
   Great Britain: 1980 steel industry,
      18-19, 61-62, 66-67
   related to restructuring, 164-65
   United States, 68
Subsidies
   Germany: in restructuring, 30
   Great Britain, 118
   Japan: for employment, 146

Luxembourg, 134, 137-38
   Sweden: for job security, 152-53
Sweden
   collective bargaining in, 101-8
   employment adjustment in, 152-59
   steel industry restructuring in, 35-38
   Swedish Steel Corporation (SSAB)
      formation and strategy of, 35-38
   restructuring in, 152-53
   role in early retirement plans, 155-
      59
Sydney Steel, 15

Taranto Steel Corporation, 33
Technology
   effect on restructuring, 1
   Belgium: developments in, 24
   Germany: changes in, 95, 98
   Great Britain, 18
   Japan, 32
   United States: changes in, 22-23
   See also Modernization
Ten-Year Program (1973), Great
   Britain, 17, 59
Thelen, Kathleen, 97
Thimm, Alfred L., 97
Torrence, William O., 22
Trade Act (1974), United States, 124,
   127, 129
Trade Adjustment Assistance (TAA)
   program,United States. *See* Trade
   Act (1974), United States
Trades Union Congress, Steel
   Committee, Great Britain, 58-61, 62,
   64, 65-67, 82, 84, 117-18
Trade Unions Confederation, Sweden,
   101-2, 104
Training programs
   Belgium, 130
   Great Britain: for worker directors,
      63-64
   Japan, 152
   Luxembourg, 134, 137-38

190

Sweden, 158
See also Retraining programs
Treaty of Paris (1951), 38
Treaty of Rome (1952), 45

Ulman, Lloyd, 8
Unemployment, United States, 128-29
Unemployment compensation,
  Germany, 139, 141, 142-43, 144
Unemployment insurance (UI)
  in Belgium and Luxembourg, 130
  Germany, 159
  Japan, 146
  United States, 124, 129
Unions
  in adversarial and cooperative
    systems, 8, 82-8, 111
  in cooperative countries, 85
  criteria for effectiveness, 165
  power of steelworker and
    metalworker, 1, 3
  Belgium-Luxembourg, 27, 87-90
  Canada, 55-56, 82
  Germany, 90-99, 139-40, 164
  Great Britain, 57-67, 82
  Japan: firm consultation with, 147
  Sweden, 35-38, 101-8, 152-59, 164
  United States, 67-82, 84
  See also Employee participation
United States
  collective bargaining in, 67-84, 124
  employment adjustment in, 123-29
  restructuring of steel industry in, 19-
    24
U. S. Department of Labor, 127, 128,
  129
U. S. International Trade Commission
  (USITC), 126
United Steelworkers of America (USW)
  in Canadian steel industry, 56, 116
  collective bargaining in United
    States by, 67-71
Upham, M., 60

USW. See United Steelworkers of
  America (USW)

Vaisey, John, 66
Van Den Hof, Karel, 88
Vath, Werner, 29, 92
Villers, Charles, 62
Vredeling, Henk, 122

Wage
  reductions in United States, 70-71
Wages
  reductions in Germany, 139
  United States: rise of real, 68
Wagner, Marcel, 134
Wahlstrom, Bjorn, 104
Wallonia region (Belgium-
  Luxembourg)
  government subsidy to, 24-25
  strikes in, 87-88
Wall Street Journal, 19, 30, 31, 49, 111
Webb, Beatrice, 3
Webb, Sidney, 3
Williams, D. C., 56, 57
Windmuller, John P., 86
Worker directors, Great Britain, 62-67
Workers' representatives, 85, 99
Workforce, Japan, 146
Workforce reduction
  in countries studied, 159
  in steel industry, 2
  Belgium, 131-34
  Canada, 57, 114-17
  EEC countries, 39, 40, 42-44t
  Germany, 28, 96, 98, 138-39, 140-42
  Great Britain, 17, 117-19
  Japan, 33, 146, 147-51
  Luxembourg, 27, 134
  Sweden, 35, 152-54
  United States, 20, 52, 74-82, 123
  See also Layoffs
Working Life Center, 105, 107
Work rules, United States, 68-69, 78, 80